UN**SATISFIED**

Finding the life you can't stop looking for

SEAN VOLLENDORF

ISBN: 978-0-9740464-5-7

Published by CMM Press, the publishing division of the Center for Mission
Mobilization (CMM), an international Christian ministry. Mobilization.org

CMM Press
PO Box 3556
Fayetteville, AR 72702
cmmpress.org

1st Edition, 1st Imprint
c 11 08 16   m 12 02 16 18:07

Campus Ministry Today is a ministry of the CMM dedicated to equipping campus
ministry leaders worldwide in evangelism, disciple making, and mission mobilization. For more resources, go to cmmpress.org or CampusMinistry.org.

UN**SATISFIED**

FINDING THE LIFE YOU CAN'T STOP LOOKING FOR

SEAN **VOLLENDORF**

CMM PRESS

Contents

1

My Search for Satisfaction

Underneath everything in your life, there's that thing,
that forever empty (spot). Everybody has it.

— COMEDIAN LOUIS C.K.

I GREW UP IN BRECKENRIDGE, COLORADO.

One of my friends from back in the day was a guy named Eric. I'll always remember Eric because he lived in a ski area parking lot in his VW bus for most of the winter. And the dude was in high school! He had parents who had a house and loved him and wanted him home. But that's how much he loved skiing. He took the back seats out of the bus and put in a hammock. He even had this small boulder on the floor between the front seats he called "cruise control." I never knew why, so one day while I was riding with him, I asked him. He looks at me, takes his foot off the gas, and puts the rock onto the pedal. The he kicks his feet up in the air, turns his head my way and goes, "Cruise control baby."

Eric and I (and all our friends really) were all about what skiers and snowboarders call powder days. A few feet of light, fluffy snow would fall, and we would kick it at the slopes, with each one of us trying to be the first to cut fresh tracks. One day I was skiing with Eric in Utah, and snow piled so high we were able to jump from the ski lift down onto our favorite run thirty feet below. I loved the feeling of flying through the air with nothing to hold me back.

My dream was to become an Olympic ski racer. By the age of fourteen, I was on track to make my dream a reality. I traveled across the country chasing my dream. I skied the Sierra Nevadas in California, the Cascades of Oregon, the Rockies in Idaho, Colorado, Utah, and New Mexico, the Adirondacks of New England. I won ski races and ranked in the top three nationally among junior racers. I was given a Colorado Gold Card. With that card, I could ski any resort in Colorado for free. I loved hurtling down the slopes at eighty miles an hour.

One year at Breckenridge, I didn't have prom tickets for my date and myself, and I didn't have the money to buy them, so I bet one of my teammates the price of the tickets that I could jump over a chairlift cable thirty feet in the air. After spending an entire afternoon building a jump big enough to shoot me over the cable (while none of my friends helped!) I hiked up the mountain and began my descent. I had this incredibly nervous feeling in my stomach as I flew down the mountain with increasing speed, and I had one thought, "What the heck am I doing?!" But it was too late to stop.

I approached the jump and before I could change my mind, shot up into the air. All I could see in my line of sight was the cable. Just as I thought I would clear it, I stopped elevating. The cable slammed square in my chest, dropped me straight to the ground, and knocked me out cold. When I woke up, I had wet my pants and temporarily forgotten my name.

But minor setbacks like these never slowed me down. Fast was never fast enough, and dangerous was never dangerous enough. Sometimes my friends and I would hike the backcountry to ski runs almost no one in the general public had access to. But the thrill came with a cost. During a short period, five of my friends died in five separate ski accidents, all skiing slopes I had skied, seeking the same thrills I had sought. One of my friends died because he was skiing out of bounds and dropped unexpectedly eighty feet into an abandoned mineshaft. These guys were all just like me, except for one thing: their pursuit of satisfaction cost them their lives. Their deaths sobered me, but at the same time I too was addicted to the lures of adrenaline rush, speed, and risk. And like most addictions, the highs wore off quickly, and I found myself on a never-ending pursuit of the ultimate jump, the ultimate run, the ultimate day. Skiing was a thrill, but when the thrill dissipated, so did the fleeting satisfaction. I began thinking something else would have to satisfy me.

I started wondering if the right girl would give me what I was looking for. I dated several, always looking for the one who would bring me what I wanted. Eventually, I buried myself in a three-year relationship. She was sweet and cute, and she supported me in everything. But still, something was missing. I couldn't figure out what it was. The girl I thought I wanted wasn't giving me what I wanted. So one night, after watching a drive-in movie on the hood of my truck, we broke up.

I started to think maybe money would be the answer to my soul search. I've always had an entrepreneurial spirit, so my senior year of high school I started a small business with a friend. Surprisingly, it was quickly successful, and I had more money than all of my friends. Having money did something to me I didn't expect; it triggered a hunger to have more. What I had never seemed to be enough. As my bank account grew, I began to dream of the things money could do for me. Around that time I visited my uncle, and he said something that stirred those dreams. He told me it wasn't money I should seek after, but what money could buy — power. Ironically, he had money, possessions, and power, yet he didn't seem any more satisfied than I was. Even at a young age, I started to see none of these things could fulfill me. But what would? Maybe winning?

Growing up, my heroes were always professional athletes. To me, they were living the dream life. They had seemingly limitless amounts of money, women, influence, recognition, and success. I would daydream about being a professional athlete and I wondered, could athletic success satisfy me? I soon got my answer.

After winning a junior Olympic ski race, the pinnacle of my junior career and something I had worked years for, I rode home, staring out the window. I was shocked by the question on my mind: "Is this all there is?" I couldn't help but wonder if Olympic champions ask the same question. Then I got the phone call.

October of my senior year, the head soccer coach for a top five Division 1 program called me. He was calling to offer me a scholarship. I couldn't believe it. So over the next ten months, I continued to train with incredible intensity and work ethic. Maybe college athletic success would fill the void. But when I arrived on campus, I quickly learned there is always someone better. I struggled during two-a-days. I played worse than I had in years. On the fifth day of practice, before we started, the coach called me aside and told me he was releasing me from the team. Once again my search for satisfaction ended early. And something deep down told me that even if I had become the star of the team, I wouldn't be satisfied.

Companies use thousands of slogans to appeal to our desire for satisfaction. Most of them end with the same empty promise: Satisfaction Guaranteed. Why? Because marketers know everyone is searching for fulfillment. From the entertainer who thinks millions of people staring at her beauty will bring happiness, to the depressed person who makes the tragic, irreversible decision to commit suicide, all of us pursue the things we think will fulfill us.

The search for gratification can lead to a host of obsessions. Our culture is a greenhouse for growing addictions. I know a guy who can't quit getting tattoos. He spends most of his paycheck on overdone body art. I know a girl who's a "tanorexic." She keeps overdoing it at the tanning beds. She subjects her body to abuse, thinking the right skin tone will bring contentment. Teenagers and twenty somethings keep hooking up, even with the risk of disease and emotional pain. The use of painkillers is epidemic. Alcohol, food, sex, social media, video games, and more have become widespread medications for a deeper need, the need for inner satisfaction.

A girl I know just got plastic surgery. She's not alone. Record numbers of Americans are getting plastic surgery. Recently, elective operations surged over twenty million per year.[1] Do this many people really have serious cosmetic issues? Or is something deeper behind the drive to correct perceived physical flaws? I believe there is. Vast numbers of healthy people think if they had a smaller nose or smoother skin or more prominent cheeks or any other number of "adjustments," they'd be satisfied.

I saw Jeff, a college student, in the gym the other day. He was going on and on about his protein heavy diet and how much he's working out. I asked him why he was going through all of that. He didn't hesitate in his answer: "Spring break, man!" He was counting on his physique to bring him attention. If you're seeking a certain body shape to fulfill you, you might want to take a harder look at all the "beautiful" people and ask yourself, "Are they really content?"

A few weeks ago, I played a game of pickup basketball with a bunch of college guys at a local gym. I got on a team with

Shelby. Shelby is a beast. He is a great player, athletic, tall, and well-built. Between games, I asked Shelby about his life.

He was from Seattle, twenty-two years old, and said he didn't have much direction.

"How'd you end up in the Midwest from Seattle?" I asked.

"I had a girlfriend back in Seattle who started taking me to a bunch of farm parties."

He kept telling his story, but I got caught up by the phrase "farm parties." "Wait. Farm party?" I laughed. "What do you do at a farm party?"

"Oh, a farm party is actually a *pharm* party, a pharmacy party, where everyone brings pills from their home medicine cabinets to get high together."

I started cracking up. "Shelby, I was sitting here thinking, 'Kinda weird, but I guess farmers gotta party too!'"

Shelby smiled and shook his head. "A bunch of us got addicted to cotton."

I was lost again. I smiled as I pictured a bunch of farmers standing around in a barn smoking cotton.

He shook his head. "Not cotton, cotton, man. OxyContin. I ultimately got addicted to heroin. It cost me my job, my apartment, and my girlfriend. My grades tanked, so I left college and moved here, to the Midwest."

The longer we talked, the more I realized we were very similar, though we lived in different worlds. I was married with kids and had a job. He was single, broke, and broken. But we had both spent a good portion of our lives looking for the same elusive thing — satisfaction.

I work on a college campus and spend most of my time with fraternity guys. One question I like to ask the young men is, "After a weekend of partying, have you ever thought to yourself, 'Man, that was fun and all, but is that it? I mean, is that all there is?'" Almost always they will begin to admit, "Bro, I think that all the time." "Dude, me too!" "Wow, I thought I was the only one."

What does it mean to be satisfied? "To satisfy" is to quench, to adequately gratify. If something satisfies, it fulfills. It meets expectations. Whether we consciously know it or not, everyone's looking for something to meet our expectations. We're all looking to be gratified, to feel fulfilled, to find satisfaction. Yet how many people do you know who truly find it? Most don't. But everyone wants to. If you could bottle lasting fulfillment, you'd make millions overnight.

You are going to college in a time when there are more things to do, there's more entertainment to take in, more cool stuff to watch, more mind blowing experiences, and more money to enjoy (when you graduate, of course) — than any culture or generation before you. But I gotta ask you a question: With everything that's available to you, will you find satisfaction? I know I couldn't.

Owning or Getting Owned?

It started out with what I wear to school
That first day, like these are what make you cool
And this pair, this would be my parachute
So much more than just a pair of shoes

— MACKLEMORE

I feel a void. There's not a total emptiness, but I feel something's
missing. I don't think there's anyone who feels like there isn't
something missing in their life. No matter how much you ac-
complish, how much money you make, or how many cars or
houses you have or how many people you make happy...

— OLDSCHOOL COMEDIAN AND MULTIMILLIONAIRE EDDIE MURPHY

PEOPLE WILL DO ALMOST ANYTHING FOR MONEY, MY FOURTH grade self included. At age ten, my friend Cory and I rode our bikes to the park to fish. We spent a couple of hours fishing, caught nothing but moss, and got back on our bikes to head home. That's when the craziness began. I was shocked by what appeared in our path around the first corner. Two high schoolers. When you're in fourth grade, you're scared to death of high schoolers. At least I was. We slammed on our brakes.

One of them was holding something in his hand. It was paper. It was green. It was beautiful. It was four crispy one-dollar bills! My allowance was $1 a *week* at the time, so this was major wealth.

I was staring at that money when he started to talk. "Which one of you wants to ride your bike down the drainage chute, up the other side, and jump your bike out into the pond…" he paused, "… for this money?" Essentially he wanted to be entertained by seeing a ten-year-old fly for four bucks.

If one of us took the challenge, chances were good of risking embarrassment, injury, or death. I thought about it for less than a second. "I'm in!" I didn't say yes because I thought it would be fun or for a good story. I didn't even do it for the glory. I did it for the cash. The payoff would be one month's salary! Easiest decision of my life.

I'd never been to the top of the chute before. When I got up there, I realized why. It was waaaay higher and steeper than it looked from below. As I stood at the top, straddling my secondhand BMX bike, I started to think about all the bad things that could happen, the worst being I would die and not get paid.

With that thought, I lifted my feet, placed them on the pedals, and literally dropped straight down the chute. I picked up speed instantly! I lost my stomach and felt like I was going down the first hill of a roller coaster. I sped to the bottom of the chute and toward the embankment. From the perspective of standing on the ground and looking up at the embankment, it appeared to be a gently sloped mound of dirt around the pond. But speeding down toward it, the embankment suddenly became a towering vertical dirt wall! At the bottom of the chute, just before I shot up the embankment, I was compressed into the bike from the force and almost crashed. Somehow I held it together, and my high speed shot me up the slope. The embankment acted as a ramp, and before I knew it, I was cat-apulted into the sky.

I'd never jumped my bike so high before. I didn't know what to do during the long flight. So, even though I was freaking out, I started looking around and slowly peddling in the air, kind of like the boy in *E.T.* pedaling in front of the moon.

When I landed, I learned how deep the park pond...was not! I'd always assumed the muddy pond was about six or eight feet deep. If only that were the case. It was actually only about two feet deep. My tires sliced easily through the water and thudded onto the hard, muddy bottom. It was at that mo-ment that I slipped off the seat and smashed onto the bike's top bar, giving myself an agonizing shot to the cojones. I let out a groan as I slowly tipped over into the shallow water in excruciating pain.

People will do anything for money.

Everyone likes money. Two second graders were matched up in class for a mock wedding. When the question was asked, "Will you take him for richer or poorer?" the young bride re-sponded, "For richer."

In a recent survey, 92 percent of respondents said they would rather be rich than meet the love of their lives. Can you believe that? Shockingly, one in fourteen people admitted that for $10 million they would commit the ultimate crime—they'd kill somebody![1]

What's crazy is, once you begin to study the relationship between money and happiness, you find out money does not produce satisfaction. Check this out: Although we are the richest nation in history, two out of three Americans say they are not happy with their lives.[2] Do you know who some of the most bored people in the world are? Those with the most money. The truth is, people with the highest net worth often experience the highest rates of boredom. So often, in fact, therapists have dubbed the phenomenon Wealth Fatigue Syndrome. "Sufferers" often grow depressed through monotony as they move from toy to toy, house to house, vacation to vacation, yacht to yacht. You may be thinking, "Now that's the kind of syndrome I'd like to suffer under." Maybe. Or maybe not. You might want to wait until you hear Frank Pittman's findings before you decide.

Frank Pittman studies billionaires. Not millionaires. Billionaires with a "B." He lives among them and observes them. After years of research, Pittman says:

> One of the main reasons wealth makes people unhappy is it gives them too much control over what they experience. They try to translate their own fantasies into reality, and we usually don't know what's best for us. Wealth is addictive. It enticingly offers happiness, but it cannot provide satisfaction, so those who have gotten a whiff of wealth may imagine that more money will finally provide satisfaction. I have found that it's not wealth that brings the unhappiness but the *belief* that wealth will bring happiness and the disillusionment that results when it fails to do so.[3]

What's Pittman's point? It's very likely the more money you have, the more you realize how little it satisfies.

I'm pretty far from being a billionaire (I'm only short one ... billion), but I feel like I can relate to Pittman's subjects. It feels like no matter what I have, I want more — more money, more clothes, more food, nicer car, better phone, faster motorcycle, a pool. It's as if I have this built-in want for something more, something better. Most can't escape it. We think, "If I only had this or that, I'd be happy." This is the core message of all advertising. "To be happy, you've gotta have what others have." We fall into the trap of thinking one more possession will gratify and fulfill us. When multimillionaire oil tycoon John D. Rockefeller was asked how much money would be enough for him, he responded quickly, "Just a little bit more."[4]

I try to teach my kids things don't satisfy. Over the years, I've kept a graveyard of their old toys behind our shed. Any toys they've become bored with make their way to the pile. It's a tall pile. There's a laser gun, Lego set, some kind of Nerf battle-axe, old remote-controlled cars. The other day one of my kids wanted a new toy, so I took him out behind the shed to see the toy graveyard. There I am watching him as he looks at the sorry condition of virtually every toy he's ever bought. At this point, he turns to me and says the same thing he always says, "Yeah, I know, Dad, but this one's gonna be different." Yeah right.

Sometimes when they're walking around the store, I'll walk up and sarcastically whisper in their ears, "If you have *this* one, you'll have everlasting happiness for sure." "Get off me, Dad!" they groan.

Economists recently tagged the generation of those born between 1981 and 1995 Generation Broke. Gen Broke has filed more bankruptcies than any other generation, including the generation who lived through the Great Depression in the 1930s![5] Are we just bad at handling money, or is there a deeper problem? I believe we're confused about where to find true satisfaction.

One of the most well-known men in world history was a Jewish king named Solomon. He was recognized throughout the world for his unprecedented wealth. But did his riches satisfy? Amazingly, large sections of Solomon's journal have been preserved to this day.

In his journal, Solomon wrote about his wealth:

> I undertook great projects: I built houses for myself and planted vineyards. I made gardens and parks and planted all kinds of fruit trees in them. I made reservoirs to water groves of flourishing trees. I bought male and female slaves and had other slaves who were born in my house. I also owned more herds and flocks than anyone in Jerusalem before me. I amassed silver and gold for myself, and the treasure of kings and provinces. I acquired male and female singers, and a harem as well — the delights of a man's heart. I became greater by far than anyone in Jerusalem before me. In all this my wisdom stayed with me. I denied myself nothing my eyes desired; I refused my heart no pleasure. My heart took delight in all my labor, and this was the reward for all my toil. Yet when I surveyed all that my hands had done and what I had toiled to achieve, everything was meaningless, a chasing after the wind; nothing was gained under the sun.

I built houses for myself— what Solomon calls a house was more like a castle. It took Solomon thirteen years to build his own house! To put that in perspective, it took Solomon only seven years to build the national temple, which was ornate and massive. The temple was carved with stone and cedar and overlaid with pure gold! It took Solomon twice as long to build his own house. Solomon had thousands of people building his house for him, and it still took thirteen years! And this is only one of the houses he built.

Before Tiger Woods' life imploded back in '09, he became the first athlete to make $1 billion dollars. With some of that money, he bought a mansion in Florida. He paid $60 million for it. After renovations, it's worth $100 million. The house has a running track, four beautiful golf holes, a home theater, a massive pool, and it overlooks his private dock where his yacht bobs up and down on sparkling Caribbean waves.

But guess what? Tiger's house would barely qualify as Solomon's shed. Solomon's house compared far more closely to the Taj Mahal than to Tiger's mansion! When Solomon's house was completed, he hosted parties of up to 14,000 people. Not at a public venue, not at a stadium, but at his house! This is the kind of wealth King Solomon had. Solomon's journal continues: "I amassed silver and gold for myself, and the treasure of kings and provinces."

When he writes, "I amassed silver and gold for myself," it's hard to imagine the kind of wealth he's talking about. Converted to today's dollars, Solomon amassed $125 billion worth of gold during his lifetime. Solomon's gold alone would make him number one on Forbes's list of the world's richest people today. That doesn't even include his silver, real estate holdings, or livestock.

No one in the history of the world has been richer than King Solomon. If anyone could have been satisfied by wealth, it would be him. Why do I mention Solomon? Because Solomon has a unique view into the question of whether or not wealth can meet our inner longings for fulfillment. What conclusion did Solomon reach in regard to his famous riches? He writes, "I concluded that everything was meaningless, a chasing after the wind; nothing was gained under the sun."

After all his earnings, after amassing billions, Solomon had the audacity to say he hadn't truly gained anything. How could he say that? He knew from firsthand experience, riches just don't meet our thirsts.

I have a friend who recently built a 15,000 square foot house overlooking a golf course in Montana. It has a golf simulator, indoor shooting range, wine cellar, and a breathtaking view of the course from an outdoor mezzanine level. I've never asked my friend whether his home brings him ultimate satisfaction, because I already know the answer. It doesn't. It didn't for Solomon. It doesn't for Tiger. It doesn't for my friend, and it won't for you or me.

There's always going to be something bigger, something better, something that promises more. Be sure of this: Whatever it is, it never satisfies for long. How do I know? 'Cuz I'm just like you. When I look to possessions to satisfy me, they always fail. If you don't believe me, answer a few questions.

Are you completely, once and for all, pleased with the amount of money you have now? Do you tell yourself, "That's enough money. I'll never need more."

Are you thoroughly satisfied with the place you live? Are you as excited about the place you live now as you were before you moved there? Do you imagine you would be more fulfilled with a better house? Nicer car? New phone?

I do a lot of public speaking to college students. After a speech not too long ago, I met a fraternity pledge who told me an unbelievable story. His uncle had died eighteen months earlier and left him a small sum of money…three hundred thousand dollars! That in itself is amazing, but here comes the unbelievable part: He had already spent most of it. He treated some friends to a trip to Europe, bought a boat and a truck, lost some in the stock market and some in casinos, and he was sitting on the remaining $17,000. Not every college student would do what this guy did, and I don't understand how he did it. But I do know *why* he did it. He was trying to buy lasting pleasure. I've done the same thing myself.

What will ultimately meet all your inner wants? I didn't grow up reading the Bible, but some of my favorite quotes about satisfaction are things Jesus said. And he made an amazing statement about where we cannot look to find life. He said, "Life does not consist in an abundance of possessions." In other words, things will never satisfy. Things and money are not where you find satisfaction. That's not where you find life. The acquisition of possessions is not the path to feeling "full."

But what is?

You Feelin' It?

Man is the only animal whose desire increases as he is fed,
the only animal that is never satisfied.

— HENRY GEORGE

Many a man thinks he is buying pleasure
when he is really selling himself to it.

— BENJAMIN FRANKLIN

WHEN I WAS SIX YEARS OLD I WENT EXPLORING WITH MY FRIEND,
Mark, in the woods near my home. We climbed trees, dug in
the dirt, skipped rocks, and told lies. As we rounded a bend on
the trail, I noticed two men huddled over an open tailgate of a
truck. They were looking at something. One of the men called
for us to come over. Even though we were scared, we wanted
to see what they were looking at, so we walked toward them.

When we got close, the man held up a picture of something
I'd never seen before. All I could see was a lot of skin and a
woman's face. As I backed away, I saw it was a naked woman. My heart started thumping. It was frightening and exhila-
rating all at once. I still remember the guy laughing, standing
there holding the magazine. My friend and I seemed frozen

in place, confused but also intrigued by the image dangling in front of us. I felt a rush.

Then we ran away. I spent the next few years wondering when I would see such a picture again. It wouldn't be until high school.

Freshman year, my neighbor asked me to housesit. I needed money, so I agreed. As I was checking out the different areas of the home, I walked through the master bedroom to the bathroom. When I walked back out, I noticed something I hadn't noticed earlier. Above the bed hung a picture of his wife, completely nude. Although it was bizarre (Who does that?), I felt the same rush I did when I was six. In another room, I discovered my neighbor's stash of magazines.

Each time I would housesit, I would look at those magazines again and again. When I was at school, I would daydream about seeing those images. But I noticed a pattern. Each time I looked at the images, I felt less excited than I did the time before. The same pictures didn't give me the same excited feeling. At the end of six months, my neighbors moved away. But I had seen enough to experience the addictive power of porn and realize, like every other addiction, it would consume me without fulfilling me.

I don't have to tell you that today's porn is much more appealing than still shots in the back of a truck. It's also much more addictive.

Do you know who Wilt Chamberlain was? Wilt Chamberlain was famous for two things. One, basketball. He was one of the greatest basketball players of all time. And two, sex. Wilt Chamberlain used his status as an NBA star to sleep with as many women as he could. Wilt claimed he slept with as many as 20,000 women during his life. Now, I did the math once, and it works out to one a day for fifty-five years. I'm not believing it, Wilt. But there's no doubt Wilt hooked up with a ton of women.

Someone asked Wilt what drove him to sleep with so many women. Wilt answered, "I was just doing what was natural — chasing good-looking ladies, whoever they were and wherever they were available."[1] I think Wilt was looking for satisfaction.

Wilt's unique track record gave him a high degree of authority on the subject of sexual satisfaction. What do I mean? If you want to know if money satisfies, ask someone who has a pile of it. If you want to know if sexual experiences with multiple partners will fulfill, ask Wilt.

When Wilt was interviewed shortly before his death, he made a surprising statement. Check out what he said: "With all you men out there who think having a thousand different ladies is pretty cool, I have learned in my life that having one woman a thousand different times is much more satisfying."[2] Here was a guy who lived a life many young men dream about, yet he warned guys not to look for satisfaction where he did. He tried it and found it lacking.

Back to Solomon. Not only was King Solomon the Bill Gates of his day, he was also the Wilt Chamberlain of his day. He used his power to marry 700 women, not to mention his 300 live-in girlfriends. He had his choice from 1000 women every night. Solomon essentially had at his disposal willing partners of every ethnicity, height, and shape to do to him whatever he wanted. In his own words, "I denied myself nothing my eyes desired; I refused my heart no pleasure." He gave himself every sexual pleasure he desired.

Is it possible yesterday's Solomon is today's porn addict, over-exposed, over-stimulated, and unsatisfied? It seems like Solomon's words perfectly describe a lot of people's porn consumption today. Writer Davy Rothbart has written some extremely transparent articles about his own sex life. Rothbart says on many occasions he's had to fake orgasm with a woman because his overuse of porn made reaching climax during intercourse impossible.[3] He's not alone.

John Mayer is a rock god. A few years back, he did a candid interview with Playboy magazine about his addiction to pornography. Like Solomon, Mayer denies himself nothing his eyes desire. He says he sometimes sees as many as 300 naked female images before he gets out of bed in the morning. Why so many? He's searching for the ultimate experience. Said Mayer, "You're looking for the one photo out of 100 you swear is going to [satisfy you], and it still doesn't… How does that not affect the psychology of having a relationship with somebody? It's got to."[4]

Mainstream sex therapists are increasingly prescribing porn as an antidote for impotence, but is this smart? Rothbart's and Mayer's experiences strongly suggest this is a naïve approach. On the contrary, not only is the pleasure of viewing pornography not helpful, there seems to be a strong correlation between its use and sexual impotence. For the first time in history, fifteen to seventeen-year-old boys are experiencing erectile dysfunction. Pharmaceutical companies are making millions from erectile dysfunction drugs in large part because internet porn is making men impotent. While a certain percentage of men clearly face legitimate medical issues that prevent performance, it is also clear that over-stimulation has placed vast quantities of otherwise healthy men on the sidelines.

Listen to what Rothbart says: "For a lot of guys, switching gears from porn's fireworks… to the comparatively mundane calm of ordinary sex is like leaving halfway through an IMAX 3-D movie to check out a flipbook."[5] There's a sex therapist named Ian Kerner who has observed the same phenomenon. He coined the term "sexual attention deficit disorder" (SADD). Kerner says, "Just as people with ADD are easily distracted, guys with SADD have become so accustomed to the high levels of visual novelty and stimulation that comes from internet porn, they're unable to focus on real sex with a real woman."[6] Just as the ultra-rich grow bored with possessions, the over-sexed are numbed by hyper-sensual experiences.

For those like John Mayer, physiological changes take place. When a person looks at pornography, the brain releases large amounts of dopamine, a chemical released by nerve cells. Dopamine stimulates feelings of pleasure. Similar spikes in dopamine levels occur when an individual takes cocaine, meth, or other addictive drugs. As with those drugs, over time you can develop a "tolerance." If you're a frequent viewer, each time you look at porn, the brain will release a bit less dopamine. Simultaneously, the brain downgrades the *number* of dopamine receptors. Fewer receptors sensing less dopamine equals less stimulation. The predictable result is the same porn isn't as exciting as it used to be.

Normally, small pleasures in life, such as watching a sunset, being with friends, or enjoying a game, stimulate pleasure and increase dopamine production. However, when you become addicted to dopamine, life's normal pleasures aren't enough. This is why porn users almost invariably become discontent with traditional porn and begin to look at more graphic, varied, bizarre, and increasingly taboo content. Shockingly, much of internet porn today depicts rape and children. Over 85 percent of the scenes in the most popular porn movies include physical aggression toward women.[7] The goal is more dopamine release, and increasingly graphic content is the only way to get there.

For those who have developed a dopamine tolerance, regular life becomes boring and stale. They feel fatigued and depressed. If you have dopamine tolerance, eventually you alter the circuitry on your brain so significantly that you need more stimuli not just to feel good, but not to feel bad.[7] Neuroscientists have seen this same pattern in the brains of video game addicts. It's no coincidence game creators are now knitting porn and violent action together in sexually explicit video games. They're *trying* to get you addicted.

Ironically, it's not uncommon for porn addicts to feel sex-starved when actually they are oversexed. It's no different than addiction to food. One of my friends is a dietician. It's normal for her obese clients to obsess about their lack of access to food. At six hundred pounds, one of her clients told her he was stressed out because he didn't know where his next meal would come from. Crazy but true.

Maybe this is what Solomon was experiencing when he concluded, "Everything is meaningless, a chasing after the wind."

In other words, King Solomon called the pursuit of satisfaction through means of pleasure a vain exercise, comparable to chasing wind. You never catch it, and even when you feel you come close, you can't hold on to it.

But it's not just sex. All of life's pleasures tend to wear off. Their newness becomes routine, even wearisome: travel, food, comforts, parties, the college experience. Yet people cling to these things in the hope they will satisfy. As country music singer Rodney Atkins sang: "I gave up smoking, women, and drinking last night. It was the worst fifteen minutes of my life."[8] The law of diminishing returns states, "in productive processes, adding more of one factor of production, while holding all others constant, will at some point yield lower per-unit returns." Said more simply, excessive exposure yields less fulfillment, not more. The same seems to be true of life's pleasures. Multimillionaire talk radio personality, Dave Ramsey, often tells his audiences, "If you eat enough lobster, it begins to taste like soap."[9]

Ever heard of Clive Wearing? Clive Wearing is the unlucky owner of the worst known human memory. Following a life-changing illness, Wearing's short-term memory was reduced to roughly ten seconds. Whether his wife leaves the room for two minutes or two years, it makes no difference. He always welcomes her with exuberance. Often times Wearing will leap with joy and shout a greeting to his wife: "How beautiful you are! How long has it been?" For Wearing, nothing gets boring. Nothing grows stale. Everything is perpetually new to him.[10] If only the rest of us could be so easily satisfied by small, daily occurrences. For us, disinterest grows with repetition.

Life is full of simple pleasures; being mentioned on social media by someone you like, being noticed, an unexpected compliment, the smell of a new car, the feeling you get at the end of a workout, the overwhelming sense of justice when the college football team you hate loses (maybe that's just me). But if you're looking to these pleasures for ultimate, lasting satisfaction, you'll be disappointed. Your admirers move on to someone else. You forget the compliment. The new car smell fades.

Sometimes we think flaunting our pleasures in front of others will make those pleasures sweeter. Recently I visited LA and decided to take in a Lakers game with a buddy. Initially, we were just going to buy some seats in the upper deck, but through a series of fortunate circumstances, we had an opportunity to buy two seats directly behind the Lakers bench! We decided to do it. For a better view? Partly. But mostly so all of our friends could see us and because I knew it was a surefire way to make sure my phone would be blowing up all evening!

To make sure my friends and family saw me on TV, I stood up and went crazy after every single made bucket, even early in the first quarter! I looked like a complete idiot.

Some of the coaches turned around to see what this nut was getting so excited about in the first few minutes of the game. People around us must have thought I was a lifetime Laker fan receiving his final wish before he died. We notified everyone we knew. We posted pictures of ourselves leaning into the Laker huddle. Rihanna and her massive bodyguards showed up at halftime and sat two seats down from me. So I posted pictures of her and other celebrities from close range. My message to my friends wasn't so much "I'm here!" as it was "You're not." You know that feeling. We all have it. You may have done the same thing. It's as if the pleasure of the experience itself isn't enough; we have to let someone know about it. But even that isn't enough.

Hall of fame football player Deion Sanders agrees. Sanders, the only person ever to play in both the Super Bowl and the World Series, is one of the greatest athletes of any generation. Sanders talked about his pursuit of pleasure: "I had everything that power, money, and sex could give me, but it just wasn't enough. It didn't satisfy me. I was empty inside, desperately empty."[11]

The pursuit of pleasure is not the path to long-term satisfaction. I've visited the Taj Mahal. I've surfed in California. I've fished for trout in the Rockies. I've skied everywhere there is to ski. I've hang glided in Utah. I've been swimming off Thailand's gorgeous beaches. I've been to the Masters. I've golfed in Ireland. Yet even with all of these experiences, I can confidently tell you: No pleasure on earth gives lasting satisfaction. The ultimately satisfying experience doesn't exist.

At the end of his life, and after experiencing everything the world had to offer, Solomon came to a paradigm-shifting conclusion. Being a Jew, Solomon's thoughts included God. He concluded: God designed us to enjoy pleasure, but not devote ourselves to it. He gave us taste buds to savor chocolate chip cookies (and dough). He gave us a sense of smell to enjoy fresh-cut flowers. He designed our sexual organs to experience sublime pleasure. Ironically, though, when we devote ourselves exclusively to seeking pleasure, we end up feeling empty and bored, unsatisfied.

To be *dissatisfied* is to be disappointed by what you receive. For example, I'm *dissatisfied* by Burger King fries (or at least I used to be, until I and everyone else quit going there). To be *unsatisfied* is different from being *dissatisfied*. To be *unsatisfied* is to be temporarily satisfied, but not lastingly fulfilled. I feel unsatisfied by McDonald's fries because they are so good, but there are never enough to fully satisfy me. I love those things! Ironically, I love them so much that they're a great source of *unsatisfaction* for me.

I don't know if you've ever read the Bible. If you haven't, I can relate. I didn't grow up Jewish or Christian or Muslim or Buddhist or even religious at all. I grew up thinking the Bible was out of touch with the realities of our modern world. But when a friend of mine encouraged me to at least read some of it, despite a bunch of personal resistance to the idea, I finally did. And when I did, something unexpected happened — I realized it applied to my life. I didn't even want it to. It just did. When it comes to finding satisfaction, I think the Bible says some really interesting things worth considering.

For example, there's a sentence in there that talks about what people tend to do in their search for fulfillment. God is quoted as saying, "My people have committed two sins. They have forsaken me, the spring of living water, and have dug their own cisterns, broken cisterns which do not hold water." Here's what it's suggesting. Humans tend to look for satisfaction in everything but God. In other words, we pursue our own gratification by chasing after experiences instead of trying to find God. A lot of those experiences are pleasurable, but we all know the pleasure doesn't last. It leaks out like water from a broken cistern. The conclusion most people reach after seeking pleasure through experience is that experience is not where you find ultimate satisfaction.

But what is?

Hungry for Success

If I didn't swim my best, I'd think about it at school, at dinner, with my friends. It would drive me crazy.

— MICHAEL PHELPS

MY YOUNGEST SON, STONE, IS ELEVEN YEARS OLD. AS FAR AS KIDS go, he's pretty lazy. I love him to death, but the man is lazy. A while back, I walked in the living room and saw him lying on the couch. I asked him if he wanted to go for a bike ride. He goes, "Actually, I'd rather just lay around on this couch." At least he's honest.

So I asked him, "What do you want to be when you grow up?"

Without even thinking, he looks at me and says, "Fat." It was actually really funny.

Being a high achiever myself, I wanted to inspire him to be something other than fat, so I go, "Do you want to learn a musical instrument or something?" He thought about it overnight and told me the next day at breakfast he wants to learn the one you put in your mouth and hum. I'm like, "Kazoo? You don't learn kazoo! Everyone already knows kazoo! You're just born and you know kazoo. You put it in and hum!" The dude is that lazy.

So I was really excited a few months ago when he told me he

wanted to do a sport. But, then he told me the sport — Karate. My first thought was, "Noooo! Not karate! Why not do a more popular mainstream sport like baseball or lacrosse or extreme ironing (yes, that's a real sport)? Anything but karate!" I'm thinking: *We're gonna walk into the studio and there's gonna be some sixteen-year-old kid with hair over his eyes and a sword in his hand.* But he kept bugging me, so I signed him up.

When I took him to his first session, we walked through the door and before me, on the mat, no lie, stood a teenager with hair over his eyes and a sword in *each* hand! You can't make this stuff up!

On the first Monday of each month, the dojo holds tests so participants can move on to the next belt and thus earn the right to keep paying. My son is not the most coordinated little dude you've ever seen. While doing his first test, he accidentally hit himself in the face with his own fist. He managed to recover from the setback to pass the exam. He was pumped! He hugged the dojo leader. We had a party. We went out for chocolate shakes. Later that night, he slept with the new belt on his pillow. He couldn't have been more excited.

But it didn't last. The next day he was already asking about the color of the next belt. What would it look like? Would it go with the rest of his outfit? His feelings of achievement had worn off. Performance doesn't satisfy. Everyone knows it. We learn this from an early age.

Four months and three belt colors later, he's already bored with success. He asked me the other day what comes after black belt. In essence he's asking where all this is going and wondering why he's doing it. Accomplishment itself is not gratifying for him anymore.

I can relate. For years I chased satisfaction in sports. I didn't feel fulfilled until I notched a victory. When I did win, the feeling of satisfaction quickly faded, sometimes even before I got home from the field.

It's not just me. Anyone who has competed in athletics knows the satisfaction of a win wears off fast. We are always left wanting more. Just ask Tom Brady.

A journalist named Steve Kroft interviewed Brady on *60 Minutes* a few years back. At the time, Brady had won three Super Bowls with the Patriots and was MVP twice. He's been named an NFL Pro Bowler eight times. By anyone's standards, Brady has reached the pinnacle of success. But is he satisfied? In the interview, Brady has this pained expression on his face, and he actually asks the interviewer a question: "Why do I have three Super Bowl rings and still think there's something greater out there for me? I mean, maybe a lot of people would say, 'Hey man, this is what it is.' I reached my goal, my dream, my life...Me, I think, 'God, it's got to be more than this.' I mean this isn't...this can't be what it's all cracked up to be."

Then Kroft asks a compelling question: "What's the answer?"

"I wish I knew. I wish I knew. I love playing football and I love being quarterback for this team. But at the same time, I think there are a lot of other parts about me that I'm trying to find."[1]

Whoa. Just like Wilt Chamberlain on sex, Brady's testimony on being successful couldn't carry more credibility. He knows what he's talking about because he's experienced it. Excellent performance and achievement will never give long-term satisfaction. The euphoric feelings that come from high achievement dissolve. Yet so many people still strive to find lasting fulfillment from their performances. Satisfaction is elusive.

John Elway, the former star quarterback for the Denver Broncos, was asked at a press conference recently how long it took him to get over his Super Bowl losses. He answered bluntly. "I'm not over them yet."[2] Elway retired way back in 1999! After his three Super Bowl losses, John Elway *won* two back-to-back Super Bowls, but apparently it wasn't enough to satisfy him.

Here's what I've seen. People of all ages falsely believe excellent performance will lead to long-term satisfaction. A lot of college students I know think making superior grades will bring them fulfillment. Or they think they'll be happy when they get out and land the sweet job. Maybe this is you. Maybe you're looking forward to your career, and you think satisfaction will come once you have the right title. The common belief for students is that some outstanding future personal performance will finally deliver lasting fulfillment. I hate to tell you this, but it won't. Your performance, no matter how good or consistent, will never give you lasting satisfaction.

King Solomon looked to his excellent record at work to bring him satisfaction. Check out his conclusion.

> So I hated life, because the work that is done under the sun was grievous to me. All of it is meaningless, a chasing after the wind. I hated all the things I had toiled for under the sun, because I must leave them to the one who comes after me. And who knows whether that person will be wise or foolish?

Not only was Solomon the wealthiest man to ever live, having limitless pleasures at his fingertips, he was also an incredibly hard worker. No one has surpassed him in business success. And yet to him it was all a chasing after the wind. In the end, he even hated all he had worked for! In other words, all ambitions, when pursued as ends in themselves, produce only emptiness.

My wife is close friends with a college student named Hannah. Hannah searched for years to find satisfaction in her performance. She recently wrote her story for me:

"How many guys has Hannah hooked up with?" This question left me devastated. It was my junior year of college and some guy had asked my friend this question. I was shocked that my double life was being found out! I had worked hard to portray a "good girl" reputation, but apparently it wasn't working.

Ever since I can remember, I prided myself on being the good girl. My idea of a "good girl" was someone who was nice to everyone, well liked, and good at everything she did. So beginning back in middle school and high school, I strived to do exactly that. My identity was wrapped up in being seen as the best at everything. I worked extremely hard and strived for perfection in all areas of my life. I made good grades (my first B wasn't until junior year of college). I worked hard to have lots of friends. I was even homecoming queen. I was the one who was always involved in extracurricular activities in high school. Ironically, I even wanted to be acknowledged as the good religious girl, even though deep down I didn't really care about God or what He thought of me. I was all these things, but the one thing I wasn't was happy.

By senior year of high school, I was exhausted trying to keep up my good girl image. So for the first time I got drunk with a group of my friends on a camping trip over spring break. It was a blast. But the next day, I threw up a lot and told myself I would never do that again. Once back at school, people found out that good girl Hannah had gotten drunk. I was so embarrassed and told myself that I would never do that again. But I would.

I found much of my worth in guys liking me and giving me their attention. I would do anything for their acceptance. I worked hard to have the "right" body image. I ate little. I exercised a lot. I was severely disappointed when my crushes didn't show me attention. Because my performance didn't satisfy them, it didn't satisfy me either. And things were about to get worse.

Junior year of college I woke up one morning in a fog. I felt a blanket of depression suffocating me. I wanted to cry but couldn't, and I didn't know why. I had everything going for me. I had just been accepted to nursing school, I had lots of friends in my sorority, I held an officer position in my sorority, consistently had some guy interested in me, and I maintained a heavy party life, all while getting great grades. But something deep down kept telling me that I wasn't satisfied.

I quickly swept these depressed feelings under the rug and began my pursuits all over again, only this time much harder. I hooked up with more guys. I lied to my friends about who I stayed the night with, and I drank to black out several times. Occasionally after a wild night I would do something religious, such as read the Bible, trying to make myself feel better. But I never felt better. I only felt tired.

About this time I noticed something I had never seen before. I saw that my sister seemed so much more at peace and happy than I was. She basically told me that, while I was working hard to perform for everyone in my life, God was there all along, loving me and wanting me to move closer to Him.

Then I heard about something that finally brought my performance-driven, exhausting search for satisfaction to an end: God's unconditional love for me. I learned that He loved me regardless of my performance, religious or otherwise. I decided that, of all the places I could place my trust, why wouldn't I place it in God? That's exactly what I did. I finally found rest, and I found it in Him.

Stone, Tom Brady, King Solomon, and Hannah all realized what each of us needs to discover: we are not designed to find lasting fulfillment in our performance. The euphoric feelings of elite performance are short-lived. We aren't built to find permanent satisfaction in achievement.

But what are we built for?

5

Does This Make My Butt Look Big?

It's better to look good than to feel good.

— FERNANDO LAMAS

SEVERAL YEARS AGO ON NEW YEAR'S DAY, I WAS SITTING IN THE living room watching bowl games with some friends. I was checking email on my phone and noticed a message from a guy none of us had seen in a while. When I tapped on it, I started laughing out loud. Adam had sent all of us the same email. It was a picture of him in his underwear. His belly looked like it hadn't seen sunlight since the mid-90's, and it was hanging over his belt line a good ways. His hair looked awful. It was two in the afternoon, but he looked like he just got out of bed. Adam had been a star athlete in high school, but the picture on my phone screamed the painful truth that those days were over. There was only one sentence in the entire email, and reading that sentence made me laugh harder than the picture: "I'll take any of you guys on for best body by December 31st." This was Adam's "before" pic.

At first, we just laughed at him. Then, we made fun of him. Then, we joined him. All the guys Adam sent the email to are competitive, including me, and within ten minutes we had all stripped down to our undies and we were taking before pics of our own. Twelve months later we found ourselves in a hotel meeting room, tanned, sans most of our body hair, shredded muscles glistening with baby oil, posing for some amateur judges we'd recruited. Insane.

I don't think it's an exaggeration to say our culture is consumed with having the right appearance. We're surrounded by diet fads, pills, and promises. No one is immune to the marketing campaign. Last week, a seven-year-old kid told me he was going to cut back on his eating and work on his figure. What?

Plastic surgeries are on the rise. Body contouring surgeries, in which the patient undergoes reshaping of body parts, are skyrocketing. I saw an ad the other day for bicep augmentation. It said, "Wouldn't it be great to have the arms of a Greek god without the hours of pain at the gym?" Seriously? Yup. For only $9,000 you can have your biceps "contoured" to appear as if you actually work out. You Greek god you.

Do so many people have serious physical defects that can be solved only through surgery? Or is it average looking people like you and me who think if we just look a certain way, we'll finally be satisfied with who we are? I'm not saying no one should get plastic surgery. I am saying if you're counting on a certain look to satisfy you, to meet your inner needs, it's not gonna work. Why? Because despite what many cosmetic surgeons advertise, your physical appearance can never deliver lasting inner satisfaction.

Ironically, it is often the most physically beautiful who are the most discontent. Hollywood is overflowing with people looking to their appearances to bring them satisfaction. If the number of body contouring surgeries being performed in Southern California is any indication, these people are not finding it.

Although body image struggles are increasingly being identified in teenage boys, girls continue to have it even tougher in this area because society puts great pressure on females to look a certain way. No young woman wants anyone to know her weight. Put a beautiful woman in front of a mirror, and she'll find a hundred things wrong with her appearance. In front of that same mirror, put a fat, slobbering guy with hairy shoulders, and all he can do is smile, nod his head, and think, *Yeahhhh! Let's do this.*

For a lot of college students, the result of this societal pressure is people who don't give themselves any grace. They feel no room for anything but perfection. That's what happened to my friend Lauren. She fought anorexia for years. This is her story:

> In early high school, I made a goal to become the best cross country runner on my team. This goal was originally a good idea, and it led, of course, to lots and lots of running. As I trained, I realized that I was getting smaller. Even though I'd always been an average size and had no health reason to lose weight, running caused me to shed some pounds. The result was that I began to receive compliments from others. I enjoyed these newfound compliments, and I wanted to experience more of them. Over time, I got addicted to the encouragement.
>
> Inevitably, I began an exhausting life on a proverbial, and literal, treadmill. I started exercising for hours a day and obsessively counting calories. But no matter how much weight I lost, it was never enough. I still felt fat. I still felt like me, my old self, but really I wanted to be someone else. Ironically,

the more weight I lost, the emptier I felt.

I spiraled into a classic case of anorexia that landed me in the hospital by the end of my junior year. Even at my lowest weight, I would have said I was not fully satisfied with how I looked. I was determined to have the "perfect" body, but I never was willing to define what that meant. Yet even at a weight so low that I was in danger of losing my life, I felt far from perfection in every way. The body I thought would satisfy me just left me wanting something more. I knew that whatever temporary satisfaction I experienced somehow wasn't going to last. I felt trapped. Either I would eventually gain the weight back, which was my biggest fear, or, if I truly wasn't able to stop, I'd die trying to reach an unattainable ideal body. Either way, I would lose.

Just before I went to college, I met a friend who seemed very secure. This was attractive to me because I wasn't. He was in debate, and one time everyone ganged up against him on an issue. I remember watching him handle himself with poise and confidence. He was kind, but he was bold, and he didn't back down when they challenged him. He didn't need other people to accept him in order to feel accepted. I was amazed and refreshed. I had never seen anything like that before. The more time I spent around him, the more attracted I became to the peace he had in his life. He seemed to feel accepted, especially accepted by himself.

I started asking him questions about the peace he seemed to have. To be honest, I had no idea what he was going to say. Eventually I learned his secret to contentment, but beforehand I couldn't have guessed what it was.

I listen to Lauren's story and feel great sympathy for what she went through. I know most people haven't felt it as deeply as she did, but haven't we all felt the sting of dissatisfaction with the way we look?

Are you searching for a certain look to satisfy you? It's unattainable. Are you looking for a certain body shape to fulfill you? You won't find it. You can diet. You can exercise harder. You can keep changing your appearance. It won't satisfy.

But what will?

Disease to Please

*I can't tell you the key to success, but the key to fail-
ure is trying to please everyone.*

— ED SHEERAN

MY WIFE AND I HAVE A FRIEND WE BOTH ADORE. SHE'S A SWEET-
heart, and we love having her around. There's only one thing I
don't like about her: the way she treats her son.

The last time I saw her, I straight up told her I don't like
how she takes care of him. She feeds him. She checks on him
while he's sleeping. She does his laundry. She cleans up after
him. She waits on him non-stop. You might be thinking, "It
actually sounds like she treats her son really well. What's your
problem, Sean?" Here's the problem. Her son is six foot three
and weighs 230 pounds. He's twenty-four years old! He's lazy.
He has no source of income. He hangs out with his friends
and gets drunk, and then he comes home to his mom, who
does everything for him. She pays his bills. She looks after him
when he's intoxicated. She handles his conflicts. The dude has
never grown up.

I keep telling her to throw him out of the house. I've even
coached her on how to go about it. But here's the deal. I'm doing it in vain. She's not gonna throw him out. She doesn't want

to. Why is she doing all of these things for an adult son? I'm not sure, but my best guess is I think she wants to feel wanted. Sure, she loves him. But I think she needs to feel needed. She's convinced if she throws him out, he will no longer see a need for her. The very idea hurts her. So what's the problem? She's looking to another person for satisfaction.

We've all looked for satisfaction in other people at one time or another. One friend of mine avoided returning a call to a business contact. The guy kept calling and my friend kept deleting voicemails, for seven years! He was afraid to tell him no on a deal. You know what the sad reality was? Prior to the awkward interaction, the business contact was a longtime close friend, and the lack of a return call ended their friendship. All he had to do was call back and say he wasn't interested and they'd still be friends today.

A sorority girl I know is a lifelong people pleaser. She adapts who she is to the group of people she's around. She told me the other day that she hopes the guy she likes will get drunk so he will tell her, "I love you." As shallow as that sounds, she's not alone. Millions are given to people pleasing. When you ask the people pleaser, "Who are you?" she thinks to herself, "I don't know. Who do you want me to be?" The core of people pleasing is looking to others for fulfillment. The worst nightmare a people pleaser can imagine is personal rejection, so she continues to do what others want her to do. She doesn't want to be pushed away.

Here's how it works: Someone wants you to do something that you don't want to do. But you reason, "If I don't do it, I'll be rejected. I'd rather do this thing I don't want to do than be rejected, which I *really* don't want to experience."

Every college student has experienced agreeing to something he really didn't want to do. Someone wants you to take notes so they can skip class. Your boss wants you to stay later.

Your girlfriend wants you to check in with her every day, or every hour of every day. But instead of saying no or voicing how you *really* feel, you agree to do the thing you don't want to do.

One of the reasons multi-level marketing works so well is because there's an abundance of consumers who are people pleasers. Multi-level marketers love people pleasers. I realize a lot of multi-level marketing products are high quality stuff, but the quality of the product is often times not the primary reason consumers buy. Companies are counting on the fact that you won't have the guts to say no to your friend who is selling to you. Last year I bought a knife for seventy-five bucks from a fraternity guy I knew who was working for a direct marketing company. He came over to my house to show me a set of knives. During the presentation, he pulls out a penny and cuts through it with the knife. It was really cool, and I told myself I was buying the knife because it could cut through a penny. But after he left, I thought, *When am I ever going to need to cut through a penny?* What the heck am I doing!? The real reason I bought the knife? I didn't want to tell my friend no. I decided to please him rather than make a good decision.

What people pleasers don't know is if you seek to please everyone you will always lose. What one person or group expects is the opposite of another person or group. When you live to please one group, you will inevitably disappoint another. So you either become a chameleon, always changing color based on who you are with, or you sell out to live for one group while disappointing others. Either way, it's impossible to please everyone!

The people pleaser's worst fear is to disappoint people, and it's usually rooted in past rejection. We've all been rejected at some point, and it doesn't feel good. Some take it a step further. They hate the feeling of rejection so much that they make a subconscious decision to do anything necessary to avoid the feeling of rejection in the future. They find themselves making decisions, saying certain words, acting a certain way, avoiding certain people, doing certain things (even good things) all because they want acceptance. They become whoever they need to become in order to gain acceptance from a particular person or group. At worst, they become approval addicts. Every decision they make, every word they say, every picture or video they post, every friend they have is driven by other people's approval or disapproval. Our culture has become a culture driven by the desire to be accepted. Self-worth is judged by who else is in your pictures, how interesting you make your life look, and how many likes you get on your most recent post. In so many ways, we've become a selfie-centered culture. Everyone is looking to gain a following to feel better about themselves.

One of my sons has Asperger's syndrome. Asperger's is a developmental disorder that involves delays in basic communication skills. One of his symptoms is social awkwardness. Because he doesn't care what people think about him, he does all kinds of things that are socially different. He laughs at sad parts in movies. He's emotionally disconnected. If I go away on a trip and return, he won't make eye contact with me because he didn't miss me in the first place.

This might sound sad to you, but there is a tremendous upside to this character trait. He has never been a people pleaser. He doesn't look to others for approval. He's not looking to people for satisfaction. He literally could not care less what people think about him. I love this about him. There are tremendous benefits to living like that. He's honest about what he really thinks. He's not trapped by the opinions of others. He's free.

One of my friends is on her fourth marriage. For decades she didn't have her own identity because her identity came from living for the approval of others. Believe it or not, I think her current marriage will survive. Why? She has finally stopped looking for a man to be her ultimate satisfaction. She's free.

I know countless college girls who believe that meeting their soul mate will solve all their problems. I hate to tell you, but it won't. People don't satisfy. Not even soul mates.

Athletes often look to the approval of others for satisfaction. Watch your college basketball team play. You can identify a freshman on the court, because when he makes a mistake, he will look over to the sideline. He wants to know what the coach thinks. He's afraid of disappointing.

Sadly, a lot of college students who look to other people for satisfaction do so because they were abused when they were younger (either sexually, physically, or emotionally). Growing up, one of my best friends was Jeff. Jeff's mom married a horrible man named Al. If Al was out of town, we would hang out at Jeff's place. If Al was home, you didn't want to go near that house. Al's favorite target was his wife. He constantly berated and ridiculed her. Even as a kid, I wondered why Ms. Anna didn't move out. Easier said than done. Victims of abuse grow familiar with the abuse and begin to believe they deserve it. It wouldn't surprise me if she had also been abused by her parents. Most people are more comfortable with old problems than they are with new solutions.

I grew up with alcoholism in my family. If you grew up in a family that abused alcohol, you know family conflict is a way of life. After I left home and went to college, I subconsciously decided I was going to avoid conflict and uncomfortable situations. I gradually started turning myself into a people pleaser. I began looking to people for satisfaction. If people were not happy with me, I would change myself to conform to their expectations to keep the peace in the relationship and to be accepted. Some people still rejected me anyway. I found out the hard way — people are fickle. Even when you do everything you think they want, they can still push you away.

If you're looking to other people to satisfy you, you're going to be disappointed. No person is qualified for that role. To expect others to fulfill you is to put unrealistic pressure on them.

Satisfaction can't be found in possessions. It can't be found in pleasure. A certain look won't give it to you. You'll never find it in pleasing others.

Does this mean satisfaction cannot be attained? Absolutely not. Fortunately, it can be found.

What if I told you happiness is attainable? What if I told you it's been right there with you all along? What if I told you the thing you're chasing has actually been chasing you? Where is satisfaction? Let me show you.

7

The Thirst is Real

I drink because I'm thirsty.

— SHANE MACGOWAN

Stay thirsty, my friends.

— THE MOST INTERESTING MAN IN THE WORLD

THE SUMMER AFTER MY JUNIOR YEAR OF COLLEGE, I WAS TRAVEL-ing in Eastern Europe with some friends, probably because we couldn't afford Western Europe, or anywhere really. It was super hot this one afternoon, and my friend Jeff wanted someone to go on a run with him. To be honest, I hate running. On a list of things I like doing, running falls just above sitting next to the guy on a plane who takes his shoes off and gives himself a slow, deep tissue toe massage in your face. So as soon as I saw Jeff put on his running shoes, I picked up a book and acted like I was reading. I guess he saw me, 'cuz he immediately singled me out. "Come on man. Let's go."

"Uh, let me think about it. No."

But after a couple insults and a challenge to my manhood, I was in. So with zero preparation, I threw on my shoes, and we headed out the door.

The trail we ran on was beautiful, but the running was actually worse than breathing some guy's stinky foot fumes at close range. After about thirty minutes, I realized something was wrong. I looked beneath my feet and the path wasn't there anymore. I couldn't even remember the last time I saw the path. Who knows when we left it, but we were definitely lost.

Then something worse happened. I started feeling thirsty. I realized I had gone out for a run on a hot day in the middle of summer, and I didn't bring any water! At that point, we started frantically searching for the path, and with every minute that went by, my thirst increased. Twenty minutes turned into forty that eventually turned into ninety.

Two hours in, we finally came out of the woods, but there was no sign of our apartment or even the town. My skin stopped sweating and went cold and dry, which is what happens when you're dehydrated. By now I'm freaking out.

Then, out of nowhere, I saw something amazing. In the distance, a truck was driving toward us. We're saved! I saw this guy in the back of the truck and, of all things, he's standing on top of a pile of watermelons. I'm like, this could not have worked out any better. Then, he bends over, picks up a melon with both hands over his head, and lobs it toward us. It floated through the air in slow motion. I reached out my hands to catch it and my mouth involuntarily opened up as if I was gonna swallow it. Then, as the melon fell toward my face, it vanished. It was a hallucination! The truck. The man. The watermelon. Gone. When I came to my senses, I got scared. Jeff and I were overcome with dryness. All we wanted was to satisfy our thirst.

Thirst is a strong, driving desire for a given substance. All of us have felt what it's like to be thirsty. And as important as satisfying our physical thirst may be, I've found there's a deeper thirst in life that's even stronger and more important — spiritual thirst.

I know not everyone is into spirituality. I definitely wasn't when I was growing up. But as I look back, I realize there was always some kind of desire in me, almost like a soul thirst. A lot of college students, even atheists, have told me they've felt the same thing.

For twenty years, I've traveled the country speaking to college students, and also listening to them. Here's what I'm convinced of. College students are looking to satisfy their spiritual thirst from an endless supply of sources.

Sometimes it's as simple as trying to satisfy soul thirst with material things. I know a sorority girl who turns to her drug of choice to feel better on days when she's down — shopping. Even though she's racked up thousands of dollars of debt on her credit cards, she keeps doing it. She's not alone. For tons of Americans, retail therapy is the fountain of healing on a bad day. Thirsty.

Sports fans are dry too. After each of the last several Super Bowls, the losing team's home city has seen severe spikes in porn site visits.[1] Disappointed fans are looking to drink from porn for comfort. Thirsty.

My best friend in high school was a stud. Incredible guy. He was smart and a great athlete. He loved everyone, and was loved back. In sixth grade, he would walk five miles one way to my house so we could have epic one on one wiffle ball matches. He would make sure special needs kids in our class got their food to the lunch table without spilling. Amazing dude. My senior year of college I picked up my phone and heard the worst news of my life. My friend had taken his life. I was devastated.

I fell to my knees and cried. My best friend had chosen a long term solution for a short term problem. That was the saddest day of my life.

Later I had time to process his death. Honestly, I could only offer weak guesses as to why it happened. But as I look back now, I think he was thirsty.

For the first time ever, suicide has surpassed car accidents as the number one cause of injury-related deaths in America. How sad is that? In a nation that has everything, so many are finding life offers nothing. Nothing satisfying anyway. Thirsty.

Ever been thirsty? So dehydrated that thirst seemed to consume you? When Jeff and I finally found water on our run, it was a dirty puddle on the side of the road with motor oil rainbows all across the surface. I didn't care though. I got on all fours and started lapping it up. I drank a mixture of water, motor oil, and mud. I was so desperate, it actually tasted good. But that's what you do when you're desperately thirsty. What's hilarious and ironic is, ten minutes after I drank from the puddle, we crested a hill and there was a kiosk with a guy selling bottled water, no hallucination this time. I got diarrhea for a week from the mud puddle water!

In the Jewish scriptures, one of the authors wrote a prayer to God: "As the deer pants for streams of water, so my soul pants for you, my God. My soul thirsts for God, for the living God. When can I go and meet with God?" Here's a question for ya'. If the thirst we experience is actually spiritual thirst, why is it most people don't talk like this? No one says, "My soul thirsts for God." Is it because our need to drink from God isn't real? I don't think so. It's that our *felt* need is *not* God. We feel we need other things to satisfy us. People don't generally go to God to satisfy their thirst. We place our hope in sports teams. We go shopping. We drink from porn.

I've got a new addiction, Coke Zero. Nutritionists and common sense tell me it's not what my body needs. I know intellectually it's not going to satisfy me, but it feels cold going down, so I tell myself it's going to satisfy my thirst. One problem with Coke Zero is it's a diuretic. Ever heard of a diuretic? A diuretic is any substance that tends to increase the discharge of water from the body. So while Coke Zero may seem to satisfy my thirst, it actually strips my body of water. Diuretics satisfy you for a short time, but in the end they leave you wanting more. Diuretics don't rehydrate you. They actually *de*hydrate you.

I think all college students feel spiritual thirst. But they usually quell their thirst with spiritual diuretics.

To quell is to suppress or pacify. Quell is different than quench. To quench is to permanently satisfy a thirst. Coke Zero quells my thirst. Only pure water quenches.

A while back, a woman was rushed to the doctor for heart problems. She said she constantly felt lightheaded and even fainted a few times. After a bunch of questioning, the doctors finally discovered a shocking fact. For the previous sixteen years of her life, this woman drank nothing but carbonated sodas. She gave up on water at age fifteen![2] Can you imagine the kind of damage she did to her body?

When you try to satisfy your physical thirst with diuretics, the results are predictable. The same is true when you try to satisfy your soul thirst. Here's what I've come to believe. God is the only one who can truly satisfy. Can thirst for God be quelled by things other than God? Definitely. Quenched? No.

The never ending search for satisfaction leads us to tell ourselves the "if only" lies. If only I could graduate and take some time and travel, I'd be happy. If only my team could win the national championship; if only I could get into a certain fraternity; if only I could get with him; If only I had a smaller this or a bigger that. And it doesn't end in college. When you get out, people all around you will have the "if onlys." If only I wasn't trapped in this marriage, then I'd be happy; If only I could hit my sales goal, I'd be content. If only ... then I'd be satisfied.

But here's what I wish I knew in college; more of something doesn't equal satisfaction. It only creates more hunger. Have you ever met anyone who eats and then thinks, "Okay, now that I've eaten, I never need to eat again?" Or, "Okay, I've had sex. I never need to do that again. I'm permanently satisfied?" Ever met someone like that? Nope. Neither have I.

I grew up thirsty. To satisfy my thirst, I did what everyone else was doing. I drank.

I drank from sports, relationships, girls, grades. I even did some actual drinking. Beginning in fourth grade, I worked as a dishwasher in a restaurant near my house. When my shift was over, I'd go into the walk-in cooler and slip a beer into the bottom of the trash can, underneath the bag. When I got outside to empty the trash can, I'd sit behind the dumpster and drink.

But drinking these things never satisfied my thirst very long. I was looking so hard to find my purpose in life — to find satisfaction — but everything I tried was a spiritual diuretic. It satisfied for a moment, maybe for a few days, but ultimately left me disappointed. My thirst was never quenched.

Then I met Tim. Tim was my ski coach. He was the ultimate man's man. He could fix anything. He was rebuilding a two-seater Alfa Romeo sports car in his garage. He coached the U.S. Ski Team, raced boats, rode motorcycles; he was a pilot, an incredible cyclist, and raced hang gliders. I didn't know this was even possible! Tim was kind to people but tough on his athletes. He was confident and driven. He seemed to know his purpose. He also claimed he found his satisfaction in God. I remember thinking to myself, "Tim is such a stud. If only

Tim wasn't religious, he would be the ideal man." Tim was everything I wanted to be. But he wasn't drinking anywhere near where I was drinking.

As we drove to ski races Tim would teach me "leadership lessons." His examples always came from some ancient kings in the country of Israel. I had no idea at the time he was teaching me, among other things, about Jesus. I probably wouldn't have listened had I known. But the stories were compelling, and I wondered where all these amazing principles were coming from.

As I watched Tim live his life for a couple of years, I began to realize his confidence came from his relationship with God. He found purpose in life from a higher power. *Tim was satisfied.* And the more I read the sayings of Jesus, the more I thought God must be what I needed too. For example, Jesus once said, "If anyone is thirsty, let him come to Me and drink." Just before I started college, I believed for the first time that "anyone" included me.

Let me tell you a secret no commercial, no celebrity, no billboard will ever tell you: Nothing in this world will satisfy you ... for very long. Not a boyfriend, not a girlfriend, more money, the right sorority, the right group of friends, a change of scenery, getting married, the right body, drunkenness, sobriety, seeing your political candidate elected, a better career. Those things might quell your thirst for a short time, but in the long run none of them will satisfy permanently.

Why not? Because the thirst you feel is actually spiritual thirst. I believe it can be satisfied only by God.

Ultimately, we all disobey God by looking to things other than Him for satisfaction. The result is that we end up disconnected from God. As I mentioned, I grew up an atheist. I didn't believe in the existence of any god. In high school, I wondered about my purpose on this earth. When my head hit the pillow at night, I'd wonder why I was even alive, and what purpose I was supposed to serve. Am I just here to play sports, study hard, and hook up with girls? Over time, I started to conclude there had to be a Creator. But what would He want to do with me? Even though I now believed in His existence, I felt so far from God.

That's when I found out about a dude named Augustine. Augustine was this Italian who grew up somewhere in Italy and far from God. For most of his life Augustine sought satisfaction in women and wine. And, like all of us, he was never fulfilled. After his college years, he finally found a relationship with God. Amazingly, he would come to be known as Saint Augustine. A few years after discovering God, he wrote some really insightful words: "You have made us for yourself, and our hearts are restless, until they can find rest in you." [3] In other words, outside of God, our thirst can be quelled but never quenched.

Solomon, the king I mentioned earlier, is also famous for his drinking. He drank from women. He drank from wine. He drank from wisdom. He drank from work. But none of his drinking quenched his thirst — until he took one final drink. One day near the end of his life, as he was reflecting on all he had experienced and acquired, he took stock of what it all had done for him. And he wrote these thoughts in his journal, "Remember your Creator in the days of your youth."

In other words, don't wait until you're older to connect with God. Do it now.

Crazy. Despite his fame, being surrounded by beautiful women, his world-renowned wisdom, his exquisite work, and his exorbitant wealth, he tells people to look away from all those things and to look to a relationship with God for satisfaction. Solomon realized something most people don't. He realized satisfaction is not a *what* but a *who*. I've come to believe this *who* is Jesus.

Remember what Jesus said? "If anyone is thirsty, let him come to me and drink." He also said, "Whoever believes in me … rivers of living water will flow from within them." Jesus was basically saying He is the one who can satisfy our thirst permanently. His quenching is not something we have to chase down. When we place our trust in Him, fulfillment comes from inside of us because He will be living inside of us. To me, the question became, Sean, will you trust your Creator to fulfill your deepest desires, or will you continue to chase after the things around you, knowing that, in the long run, they won't satisfy?

Misconceptions

So many people, you gotta make exceptions, 'cuz,
they look at you with misconceptions.

— HIP HOP RECORDING ARTIST CHOO JACKSON

I'VE LIVED LONG ENOUGH TO REALIZE NOT EVERYTHING IN LIFE IS what I initially think it is. That was the case with Chad Jordan, a seventh grader who played football in the Tampa Bay Youth Football League. Everyone loved Chad. He was liked by his teammates and coaches, and he was a dominant football player.

But something wasn't exactly right. His coach was the first one to notice. After practices, Chad wore his helmet for the entire team meeting and kept wearing it later when he walked home from the field. Other people noticed Chad didn't look like your average seventh grader. Let's just say he looked a little older. After some investigation, authorities were shocked at what they found. They realized Chad Jordan, the seventh grade football player, was not Chad Jordan at all. He was actually twenty-one-year-old Julious Threatts, a full grown man.[1] What? No wonder he dominated! Not everything in life is what we initially think it is. In other words, sometimes we have misconceptions.

I heard about some college students who played an awesome prank on one of their friends. During spring break, students literally turned their friend's room upside down. A group of twelve took hundreds of screws and attached the bottom of Aaron Miller's bed and desk to the ceiling. Yes...the ceiling! They then suspended books inside the desk shelves with staples and used fishing line to give clothes in the closet the appearance of hanging *up* from their hangers. In every way, the room appeared as if gravity was working in reverse. When Aaron returned from his spring break trip, he was amazed and confused. He had no idea what had happened or how. When he finally realized he hadn't lost his mind, he thought it was hilarious. He nearly collapsed falling out laughing.[2] It was an incredible prank. Aaron Miller realized not everything in life is what we think it is.

When we think something is one way, but really it's another, it's because we have a misconception. What if a bunch of your friends started saying untrue things about you? Imagine if people were saying you had stolen something or you dealt drugs or you got a Bieber tattoo. You would be offended. I would too if it happened to me. Unfortunately, I think this happens to God all the time.

Not only do we have misconceptions of people, we also have them of God. The difference is no one challenges you when you voice misconceptions of God. Have you noticed that? I could say something crazy about God, like, "God is whoever you want Him to be," and no one would challenge my statement. No one's gonna speak up and go, "Is He though? Is God whoever you want Him to be? Or is this a misconception of God that needs to be corrected?"

Thing is, there have always been misconceptions of God, going all the way back to Jesus. I remember reading one time about a conversation Jesus had with one of his followers, a dude named Peter. Jesus knew there were a bunch of misconceptions out there about himself, so one day he straight up asked Peter, "Who do people say I am?" In other words, "What are people saying behind my back? Who do people believe me to be?"

One thing I've learned is it's super important that I have an accurate conception of God. Why? Because my conception of God will determine where I look for satisfaction. Some guy in India married a dog a while back. He had killed two mating dogs for sport and felt terrible about it. So he asked his village religious leader what he should do. The leader told him the way to deal with his guilt was to marry a dog. So he did.[3] Seriously? How is this possible?

This guy believed God is someone who makes you perform an act to pay for your wrongdoing and relieve yourself from guilt. His conception of God determined how he dealt with his misdeed. Do I think he's right? No. Do I think he found satisfaction? Uh, no. My point is his conception of God is determining how he's living his life, and it's determining whether he finds satisfaction.

I've come to the conclusion college students miss out on finding fulfillment in God because they have misconceptions. How can you find fulfillment in God if you don't know what He's like? We have to identify our misconceptions. Do you know who God really is?

On-Demand God

I like vending machines 'cause snacks are better when they fall. If I buy a candy bar at a store, sometimes I will drop it so it achieves its maximum flavor potential.

— MITCH HEDBERG

I USED TO THINK JESUS WAS LIKE SOME KIND OF ON-DEMAND GOD. Now I know that a god who gives you everything you want is like a bad parent who doesn't really love you.

I had this friend in fourth grade named Jess. Jess was a cool guy to hang out with. We both liked football, video games, and girls, in that order. One day, Jess invited me over to his house. Even though I had known Jess for about six months, I had never been to his place. As it turns out, I only went once.

When I got to his house, I noticed immediately he seemed like a different person. He opened the door, but his back was to me, and he was yelling at someone inside. He was screaming actually. He was swearing and telling someone inside what to do. I found out a couple minutes later who that someone was. It was his parents!

At my house, if you screamed at your parents, you lost your house. But here's what's crazy. His parents didn't do anything about it. Even worse, they actually did whatever he told them to do. Even at that age, I knew this was not how you parent a kid. After an hour, I was ready to bail on Jess' place and on our friendship. So I did.

It would be really nice if God responded to all our requests by doing exactly what we want him to do, like give us money or better grades or satisfaction, but Jesus didn't really interact with people that way. I think it's because he's way wiser than I give him credit for. He knows there are things we want that wouldn't really be beneficial for us to have.

I think a lot of college students think of God like I did, as some kind of on-demand God that plays the exact show you program him to play. I love on-demand entertainment options. You find what you want. You watch what you want. No commercials.

But God's not an on-demand God. I can't tell Him what I want and, as long as my request is reasonable, expect Him to make it happen.

How do I know? Good question. How can we know what God is really like? How do we get an accurate conception of God? I go to the place that reveals Him most clearly — the sayings of Jesus. Jesus said God is the exact opposite of an on-demand God. Instead, He's first and foremost a Father.

He once said, "Which of you, if his son asks for bread, will give him a stone? ... If you, then, though you are evil, know how to give good gifts to your children, how much more will your Father in Heaven give good gifts to those who ask him?" In other words, God is our Father. If you want something, don't demand God do it. And don't do religious things so you can "warm God up" or put Him in the mood to give it to you. Instead, just ask Him. He's a living being who wants to have a satisfying, life-giving relationship with us.

When we view God as an on-demand God, He can be reduced to a good luck charm. When my wife was in junior high, she had an eight by ten painting of Jesus on her dresser. She didn't really believe in Jesus, but she wanted him around for superstitious reasons. What's hilarious is she would turn the picture around when she changed clothes. We can't have Jesus looking at us while we're changing, now can we?

Jesus said God does things for us just because He's our Father, and He loves us. He doesn't want to be our little good luck charm we rub for things to go well in our lives. What kind of a relationship would that be? What if your closest friends never talked to you but just walked by and touched your head for good luck? That would be sad, not to mention insanely weird.

But I talk to so many college kids who think if they do certain good things, such as going to church, helping a friend, attending a Bible study, or donating money to a good cause, they will get specific things out of God. A guy told me last week, "I'll do something religious ahead of time so I can do well on my exam." Another guy told me he goes to church so he'll play a great baseball game. On-demand God.

I've been a father for a while now. One of my favorite things is to be with my boys, just hanging out with them. I love it.

My middle son, Sim, is adopted. He was born in India. I'm crazy about this kid. Very funny guy. When he was nine years old, he wasn't that into sports. One afternoon I was trying to get him to throw the football with me out in the yard. He had zero interest, but I kept asking. Finally, he looks at me and goes, "Dad, face it, I'm a nerd," and walks off laughing.

Even though I'm crazy about my sons, they occasionally do things that bug me. For example, they sometimes treat me super nice so they can get something. Sim recently went into this monologue about me being the best dad in the neighborhood.

At the end of the speech, he made his request. "Dad, can I stay at Jacob's house tonight?"

I was ticked. I stared at him for a few seconds. Then I said, "Are you really gonna warm me up with fake compliments just so you can ask for something? Do you know how much that cheapens our relationship? It's an attack on my character. It's as if you're saying, 'Dad, you probably don't want to do something good for me just because you love me, so I'll say some nice things to you to warm you up.'" He just stared at me. Then I smiled and let him go.

My kids need to be reminded I'm their living father, not some on-demand machine. The same goes for God.

Last week I bought ice cream for my youngest son. On the way home, I asked him, "Do you know why I did this?"

He looked up at me with ice cream on his face and said, "Yup. Because I obeyed today."

"Nope."

"Because I did good on my spelling test?"

"Nope."

"Because I passed my karate test?" I laughed.

"No, I kinda wish you'd quit karate. I'd rather watch a football game." He laughed.

We walked a little bit further and then he looks up at me and goes, "Then why?"

I smiled and said, "'Cuz I love ya, man. You don't have to *do* anything. I love you already. I want to do things for you because I love you. And, sometimes I'm gonna say "No" to you because I love you. Either way, I love you."

I've learned it's not satisfying to cheapen my relationship with God by turning Him into an on-demand God. I gotta think He knows if He always gave me what I want, I'd turn into Jess, demanding and bossy and ungrateful. Something tells me that deep down Jess didn't want that kind of relationship with his father. Jess wasn't satisfied.

10

Party Pooper God

God is great, beer is good, and people are crazy.

— BILLY CURRINGTON

I USED TO THINK FOLLOWING JESUS WOULD MEAN GIVING UP LIV-
ing a fun life. But the more I learn about him, the more I'm
convinced he was an extremely fun guy.

A few years ago, I led a spiritual discussion group for some
fraternity guys. The first night, I asked this question: "What
would this Greek chapter be like if everybody here lived like
Jesus?" I expected someone to say everyone would be humble.
I thought maybe someone else would say the guys would be
serving one another and putting others' needs ahead of their
own. Or something along those lines. I expected wrong. Instead, one of the guys said, "Man, that sounds awful. Everything would be so boring around here."

One week I brought a book to the group called *One Thing
You Can't Do in Heaven.* The book is actually about helping
people find a relationship with Jesus. One of the guys, John,
saw the book in my hand, so I asked him, "John, what do you
think is the one thing we can't do in Heaven?"

John thought for a minute and then said, "I don't know. I guess I've always thought there are a *lot* of things I can't do in Heaven." I laughed. His response was funny to me, but also revealing. He obviously thinks God is a party pooper, and that Heaven isn't going to be satisfying.

I've found that a lot of college students have this misconception. A student I know told me, "I thought if I followed Jesus I'd end up a minister and then have to marry some woman who's a stiff." Funny thing is, he's now a minister. And his wife's a stiff! Ha. Just kidding. He sells insurance, and he's single.

Honestly, though, I think Jesus has a PR problem. It's not his doing. It's his people who have earned him a bad rap. A lot of people who claim to know him *are* stiffs. They don't live or laugh or joke or embrace life. And instead of serving others and helping others achieve their dreams (both major keys to happiness), they seem to look down on people who have different values. In the words of an old guy I met late one night at Walmart, they act like their poop don't smell. Maybe that's why they don't mind being party poopers.

There were a lot of people like this in Jesus' day too, overly religious people who think they're morally better than everyone else, but don't really care about anyone else. Jesus actually ridiculed people like this for taking pride in their religiosity. These type of people constantly criticized Jesus for spending time with "sinners." In their minds, a sinner was someone whose actions and choices placed them at odds with the ones who considered themselves morally superior.

Jesus was the exact opposite. He laughed, told jokes, gave his friends a hard time, and made fun of people who took themselves too seriously, especially people who considered themselves religious but weren't truly loving toward other people.

Jesus is no party pooper. He even turned some water into wine to keep a party going. The more I learn about Jesus, the more I'm convinced everyone would want him as a close friend.

One time Jesus was telling a bunch of people the reason for his mission on earth. He said, "I have come so that people may have life, and have it to the full." In other words, he didn't come for himself. He came for others. And his claim was really bold. He was saying the richest, most satisfying life people can experience is found in a relationship with him.

I was talking to a guy on campus last week. We were talking about finding satisfaction in God. He told me, "I'm gonna wait 'til later to make my spiritual life a priority." Basically he was saying he thought he could find more satisfaction in college if he put Jesus off for a while. I understood where he was coming from. That was exactly how I used to think. I could relate to the pastor who said, "I used to not want to glorify God... For example, I don't want to be a virgin. They make movies about people who are virgins, and they're comedies. I don't want that. That's not what I'm shooting for."[1] Funny but true.

The main reason I didn't start following Jesus sooner than I did is I thought I would have to give up things I enjoyed. I didn't want God to turn me into some saintly do-gooder who didn't know how to have a good time. I thought this because a lot of the religious people I knew actually *were* boring. They were party poopers, so I thought they followed a God who also was.

But then I read one of the most surprising teachings of Jesus. He said, "Whoever wants to save his life will lose it, but whoever loses his life for me will find it." I always thought the way to find happiness was to find things that made me happy and then hoard them. In other words, when I pursue a life trying to find satisfaction for satisfaction's sake, what I actually end up with is emptiness and discontentment. But when I "lose" my life for the sake of other people by serving them, loving them, helping them achieve their dreams, I actually find fulfillment.

I've come to believe life following Jesus is actually the most interesting, enjoyable, fun life one could imagine. God is not some grouchy being in Heaven whose sole goal is to make sure we don't have any fun.

Sometimes I just sit back and think about the enjoyment we experience in this world! It comes from God! God equipped the human body with the capacity to enjoy pleasure. He gave us eyes to appreciate sunsets. Sunrises, too, but I haven't seen too many of those.

Who is the genius who thought of sex? God. God created the first man, Adam, and then put him down for a nap. (For that matter, who created naps? Naps are amazing!) When Adam wakes up, there's a naked woman standing there. And then God says, "Be fruitful. Multiply." I don't know about you, but I'd be saying, "God is good! Let's party!" This is the only command the human race has obeyed, by the way, "Be fruitful and multiply!" Question: Who do you think created orgasm? The most emotionally powerful, spiritually binding, and physically pleasurable act someone can experience came from the mind and generosity of God. All God's idea.

A guy told me last week, "When I finally stopped believing the misconception of God as a party pooper, my life took off. Before I started following Jesus, I had many great times with my friends. But a lot of my fun led to barely remembering what happened the night before. Once I started to find my satisfaction in God, I began to learn that there's sinful fun and nourishing fun."

I've learned God has a reason when He tells me to not do something. Whether it's sexual activity outside of the commitment of marriage, not forgiving those who wrong you, having a racist heart, or doing drugs, sinful fun does something I'd never expect. It contaminates your soul. God wants to protect you from that pain. How many of us have regrets that are tied to something we did the night before? If I'm seeking lasting happiness and joy outside of God's loving parameters, I won't find it.

So many times, I talk with college students who think they'll be missing out if they decide to follow Jesus, that somehow they'll be overly constrained and not be able to experience freedom. I get it. I used to think the same thing.

I looked at our hookup culture and wondered why Jesus isn't ok with it. I mean, is he trying to box us in? Then I realized Jesus isn't a prude. He invented sex in the first place.

Is it possible Jesus knows something we don't? Could it be he's wanting to protect us from regret and from hurting others? I don't mean to sound like some preacher, but in talking with thousands of college students over the last twenty years, and after watching so many of my friends in their late twenties divorce, I think our hookup culture is hurting people, not helping them. Jesus saw this long before I did.

We can learn a lot from a fish. A while ago, one of our friends gave us a pet fish. The fish was dark blue. Stone named him Bluer because he was "bluer than blue." Who does that?

What if the fish, swimming around in the aquarium, saw all of us in the room enjoying each other and wanted to be part of all the fun? What if the fish couldn't stand to be on the outside looking in (or, I guess, on the inside looking out) any longer? What if, in a moment of curiosity, the fish jumped out of the aquarium and onto the kitchen counter? What would happen to the fish? Dead in twelve seconds. We look at the "fishbowl" of Jesus' teachings as restrictive. God sees them as protective.

Jesus isn't a party pooper. Couldn't be further from it. He wants to give you a full, rich, satisfying life.

11

Anti-Science God

Hard to find anything lovelier than a tree. They grow at right angles to a tangent of the nominal sphere of the earth.

— BILL NYE, THE SCIENCE GUY

I USED TO THINK BELIEF IN SCIENCE AND BELIEF IN GOD WERE fierce enemies, but now I realize you can be an expert in either and still believe in both.

It was a huge day for me.

It's eighth grade. Physical science class. Today, I'm gonna find out who my lab partner is. I know who I want for my lab partner. Easy. Ashlyn Moore. Ashlyn has long brown hair. She has big, beautiful brown eyes. And she's smart. To be partnered with Ashlyn is to get an A.

When partners were announced, let's just say things didn't quite go my way. I didn't get Ashlyn Moore for my lab partner. Instead, I got Mike. Mike also had long, brown hair. I'm sure Mike had beautiful eyes, too, but I couldn't really see them because his hair was covering his face. And I'm not sure if he was smart because he rarely showed up.

After about three weeks of not turning in his homework, Mike decided to come to class one day. He had some papers with him. He had actually done some work. The teacher looked at him and said, "Mike! You've turned over a new leaf." The next day, Mike showed up again with his completed assignment. He did it again the next day.

After Mike turned in his work about five days in a row, he showed up to class empty handed. When it came time to turn in our work, the teacher passed by our desk and Mike had nothing to show. The teacher goes, "Mike, what happened to that leaf you turned over?" He looks up slowly and goes, "Ehhhh, I must have smoked it." The class started laughing. I started thinking about my grade. I was beginning to think Mike already had a lab of his own.

Despite my poor lab partner, I came to love science. I'm no scientist or anything, but I love how the world around us just seems to work.

Did you grow up watching Bill Nye, The Science Guy? I love Bill. I love him because he's passionate about science, and he knows how to get other people passionate about science. He's a fairly entertaining dude, too.

One of the things Bill likes to say is this: "Science is the key to our future, and if you don't believe in science, you're holding everyone back."[1] I can see his point. Why would I not believe in science? I don't have any reason to not believe in science, especially the science we have today.

Science has come a long, long way. I think people make a mistake when they try to pit science and Jesus against each other. As far as I can tell, science seems to coexist with the teachings of Jesus. To me, they work together. In fact, I would even say that, the more scientific discoveries are made, the more science agrees with Jesus. What the heck do I mean? Check this out.

Science now tells us happy people live longer, healthier lives. So does Scripture. It says, "A cheerful heart is good medicine." Science shows us laughter actually activates immunity cells. Jesus never talked about immunity cells. I need science to explain to me what they are. But science confirms what Jesus said.

Science now says we should wash our hands, quarantine infected people, and employ proper sanitation to prevent the spread of disease. But it didn't always say that.

6,000 years ago, a couple million Jews were living in a desert as refugees for forty years! With two million people taking a dump every day (or leaving one, really), can you imagine the health risks? Yet very few people died of disease. How is that even possible? Simple. God told them to bury fecal matter and all other waste, not just flush it away but actually bury it. He also told them to quarantine infected people. Jewish law said, "As long as they have the disease, they remain unclean. They must live alone outside the camp." Louis Pasteur didn't discover germs with his microscope until 5,000 years later, so even though the Jews didn't know why they were following these health codes, they experienced the benefits.

If only 14th century scientists would have read the Scriptures. In the 1300's, bubonic plague spread across Asia, North Africa, Europe, and a lot of other places. In Europe alone, tens of millions of people died horrible deaths. And scientists couldn't figure out why it was spreading.

Pretty much everyone now agrees poor sanitation helped keep the plagues alive and killing. In those days, people just threw their trash in the gutters, and a lot of times open sewage was flowing in the streets. Also, no one knew it was important to quarantine victims, so the disease kept moving on.

Eventually, there was this Jewish doctor in France named Balavignus. He proposed miserable sanitation was a factor. He decided to initiate a cleanup movement among Jews in his neighborhood. What happened next? Most of the rats left his neighborhood and moved to the dirtier, non-Jewish parts of town. The result was Jewish mortality rates were only five percent of their non-Jewish fellow citizens.[2]

Some people say the plague eventually "burnt itself out." But it wouldn't have done that if the germs were able to keep transmitting to new hosts. Quarantine and sanitation prevented their spread. There's a professor of the history of medicine at University of Pennsylvania. Intelligent man. His name is David Riesman. He gave his opinion on the effects of this cleanup effort among the Jews: "These practices not only eliminated the plague as a pandemic menace for the first time in history but also led to general laws against infectious diseases, thereby laying the foundations upon which modern hygiene rests."[3] What's interesting to me is God had actually already laid the foundations for modern hygiene over 5,000 years earlier.

Hungarian scientists in the 1800's could have used the scriptures as well. A Hungarian doctor noticed a high mortality rate among pregnant women in his hospital. When he went to see what was going on, he noticed maternity interns were not washing their hands thoroughly after examining corpses in the morgue. And worse, some of the ones who were washing their hands were doing it in a sink full of sitting water. It was basically a cesspool for germs. From the morgue, they were going directly to the maternity ward, of course spreading disease. When he forced everyone to wash their hands after handling dead bodies, the mortality rate plummeted.[4]

Why didn't they wash their hands before? Because microscopic diseases couldn't be seen. Again, no Louis Pasteur yet. He came on the scene about ten years later. But God said way back in the day people should wash their hands with running water, not just water but running water. I don't blame the doctors in 19th century Hungary for looking to medical text books to find medical answers, but ironically, their answer was in a religious book.

Funny enough, a decade later, a lot of people in the scientific community ridiculed Pasteur when he started making presentations about germs. One journalist said to him, "The world into which you wish to take us is really too fantastic." But the world into which he wanted to take them did exist, and always had existed, microscopically.

Could it be getting to know Jesus is similar? For some, His world is just too fantastic. It sounds too good to be true. But maybe they don't have the right scope to see him. I can relate to Louis. I want to take my friends into an unseen world also.

In 150 B.C., a Greek astronomer guy named Hipparchus estimated there were 1,022 stars. Ptolemy later said there were 1,056.[5] Eventually, science and scripture got on the same page. Scripture says the stars are as numerous as sand on the shores. Scientists are now saying there are even more stars than grains of sand. Wow. When I read about new scientific findings, I become more and more amazed by the Creator of it all.

Amazingly, we have only explored under five percent of the ocean! Ninety-five percent of the ocean is unknown to every human who has ever lived. What if Jesus is like the ocean? What if you could spend millions of years learning about him and wake up one day to find out you've only discovered five percent of him? Sometimes I wonder if one of the purposes of the ocean is to illustrate how vast God is.

God isn't against science. In fact, I think He's very for it. Why are there laws in the universe? He put them there. He set them in motion. And He's been waiting for us to discover them.

There's a lot of other stuff about both science and Jesus I don't know a whole lot about. But when it comes down to it, I don't see what the fight is for. I think religious people make a mistake when they give faith based answers to fact based questions. I've found a lot of faith based answers to be intellectually lazy and incomplete. I also think scientific types make a mistake when they put all their faith in something that possibly happened a long time ago and then talk about it like it's a fact.

There's a time to read Scripture and there's a time to take medicine. Me, I just try to apply natural solutions to natural problems. The other day, the tailgate broke on my truck. I didn't pray about it. I took it to a mechanic. I didn't take it to the church so people could pray for it. If I took my truck to a church and asked the people there to pray for it, they would look at me funny and ask me why I didn't take it to a mechanic.

What's really cool to me is most of the fathers of modern science didn't see a distinction between faith and science. Galileo, Copernicus, Bacon, Kepler, Descarte, Pascal, Kelvin, and Mendel all believed in a Creator.[6]

Isaac Newton was a super famous physicist. I love what he said: "This most beautiful system of the sun, planets, and comets, could only proceed from the counsel and dominion of an Intelligent Being."[8] I also love what a super not famous friend of mine in Arkansas told me. "If you want to be amazed by all that's been created, don't sit there and read the Bible. Go out and explore." I think they're both right.

In the same way I'm not gonna be spiritual about fixing my truck, it would be a mistake for me to look at science to explain the spiritual realm. When it comes to our souls and eternity I think there's only one source we can trust, Jesus.

For a really long time, I thought I had to make a decision between trusting in the findings of science and trusting Jesus. I wondered whether science or religion was right. Answers I got from my science professors weren't satisfying. Neither were the ones I received from clergy. I'm done with the fight. To me, science is the discipline of discovering all God created. I don't feel like I have to choose between science and religion.

I don't think you have to choose between God and science. I also think it's ok to quit believing in the anti-science God. To me, that God doesn't exist. God isn't anti-science.

I believe God created the world. Everything we discover is a discovery about how God did it.

What many people don't realize is that more and more incredibly intelligent scientists are actually pointing to the Creator. Sure, there are many scientists who deny the existence of God, but there are also many scholars who have proven we don't have to choose between science and God.

I love that I can love science. And I believe it is even more enjoyable when I explore science with the perspective that I am also learning more about Jesus. As I discover things about our world and creation, I am learning how smart God is. How incredible is it that the creator of the world who wants a relationship with me also is in the tiniest details of nature? The beauty of butterflies, the harmony of insects and flowers, the tides of the ocean.

I don't look at a guy like Bill Nye and think God must not exist. I look at him and think: *That's an incredibly smart dude. He must have been be made by an incredibly smart Creator.*

Make-Believe God

I'm not an atheist. I think God is there and that he is watching and he made us. I just don't give a $@&%. I don't "believe in god." I have zero idea how everything got here. I would personally say that, if I had to make a list of possibles, God would be pretty far down. But if I were to make a list of people that know what they're talking about, I would be really far down.

— LOUIS CK

GROWING UP, I USED TO THINK GOD DIDN'T EXIST. BUT NOW I SEE Him everywhere.

When I first met my wife, Kim, I was in my third year of college. One of the first things I noticed is her height. She was six foot one. Still is. She had long, gorgeous legs — not that I noticed them. I was focused on her personality. Kim was already tall way back in junior high, taller than all her classmates, and they made fun of her. But I love her height. It's always been attractive to me. I'm just under six feet, and let's just say I'm not afraid to take a step up in the gene pool. When Kim and I began to date, I imagined one day I would wrap my arms around her, place my hands on her back, pull her in close, and kiss that girl ... on my tiptoes.

Every relationship that culminates in marriage goes through several stages. First, you meet. Either you introduce yourself or someone introduces you (or you creep on someone on the internet). Then, you tell a bunch of lies to each other to get the other person to like you. The more time passes, the more you're willing to fart around the other person. And finally, you get engaged.

Seriously, though, after you invest a lot of time getting to know each other's character qualities and find out what this person is really like, you begin to make deeper commitments to each other. Finally, when you get married, you say no to everyone else to say yes to this one person. You promise to forsake everyone else and be faithful to each other for life. Not every relationship follows this exact pattern, but a lot do.

Our relationship with God follows a similar pattern. You are introduced to Him. You check Him out. You get to know Him. And finally you commit your life to Him.

Do you remember the day you found out Santa Claus doesn't exist? I do. I'll never forget it. I finally realized the writing on the gift wrappings was the same as my mother's. I was devastated. All hope was lost. I was instantly depressed.

My youngest son didn't experience any such disappointment. Being very matter of fact, he's never had any interest in Santa Claus. Unfortunately, at recess he went so far as to tell his entire kindergarten class about Santa's nonexistence. His announcement went like this. "Guys, there's no Santa Claus. He's a fake." When he got a little attention, he went on, "It's actually the Easter Bunny that brings the presents."

For you to meet someone, one of the prerequisites is he must exist. Not complicated. If we're going to meet God, He has to exist. If you are going to be satisfied by a relationship with God, He must be real. But I'm meeting more college students these days who wonder if He's just make-believe. Which is it?

I grew up an atheist. Not only did I not care about believing in Jesus, I thought anyone who believed in Him was a weak-minded fool. They believed in a make-believe God. Later, I began to realize the existence of something was not dependent on who believed in it, even if the "who" was a stud like myself.

A few years ago, a crazy cool picture was taken from a low-flying airplane over a Peruvian rain forest. It was of tribal people. What made the picture so fascinating was that it was the first known photo of a "stone-age" tribe of Indians.

Imagine the airplane from their point of view. They may have thought the airplane to be a large bird or maybe even a god. Their world is that different from ours. Think about this: Of all the things these people believe in, there's one thing they certainly don't. You. You are 100 percent out of their reality. They've never seen a picture of you. They don't have TV or Internet. They've never Googled you. No one has ever made contact to tell them about you. To them, you don't exist.

But does this mean you don't? Of course not. All the evidence is present that you do exist. You have a name. There are pictures of you. Others are witness to your existence. The existence of something is not based on *who* believes in it.

In the same way, whether or not God exists is not based on how many people believe in Him. Or who believes in Him. Just because a person doesn't know something exists or doesn't believe it exists doesn't prove anything regarding its nonexistence. The reverse is also true. Just because someone believes in God does not prove He exists either. So what determines God's existence? Evidence.

Design Implies a Designer

When my wife was in college, one of the reasons she started

believing in God was she realized every created thing has a design. Surprisingly, she wasn't in a religion class. She was in an anatomy class. The professor was talking about meiosis, mitosis, and the development of organ systems. She was amazed at how cells could divide and multiply and then diversify to each play a unique role within an organ system, functioning as one system within the body. She walked out of class convinced there was a designer. That day was her first step toward her personal belief in God.

I was driving in western Pennsylvania and looked up on a hillside. In the snow, in perfect block letters, I read, GO STEELERS! Someone had obviously walked up on the mountain and etched those words with their footprints. What if I were to tell you the wind had written those words? You would never believe me. Why? Because an intelligent message requires an intelligent messenger. Design implies a designer.

Remember Alpha-Bits cereal? Pour out a pile of Alpha-Bits cereal on the counter and turn a fan on it. Would you expect to see coherent paragraphs emerge on the floor? It'll never happen.

Hebrew Scriptures say God's creation is God's message to us, and it's shouting to us of His creative power. One of the places God is shouting the loudest about His genius design is in DNA, which is, among other things, a message. In DNA we find a message infinitely more complex than GO STEELERS!

DNA is present in all living organisms. It's the main "ingredient" in cells. DNA is a carrier of genetic information. It's unique to each person, which is why you'd better not leave so much as one hair at the scene of a crime, because you will be convicted based on the uniqueness of that DNA sample.

Here's what's amazing about DNA. It's information. It's a language! DNA has been called the language of life, and it is extremely complex.

Bill Gates knows what he's talking about when it comes to computers. He said, "DNA is like a computer program but far, far more advanced than any software ever created."[1] And the coolest thing about DNA? It is a message. What do we know about messages? Every message has a messenger. If "GO STEELERS" implies a messenger, what about three billion units of information that build a human being? Where did the information in DNA come from? Who wrote the software? If I would never agree a message in the snow was written by wind, why would I say chance and time wrote the DNA program that creates life?

As you sit in biology class this year, notice how everything from your body to the ecosystem has amazing, coherent design. I believe intelligent planning went into the world around us. Design implies a designer.

The Laws of Physics

Several years ago, a truck driver in LA named Larry Walters strapped a lawn chair to a Jeep, tied a bunch of helium-filled balloons to the chair, settled into the chair, and then told his friends to cut the straps. It reminds me of the famous last words of every redneck, "Watch this!"

Larry wanted to float up about thirty feet into the air and then one by one shoot the balloons with a pellet gun, thus slowly descending to the ground. Instead, when they cut the straps, he absolutely shot up into the air extremely fast and high.

He topped out at around 15,000 feet! When he got too high, he started shooting his balloons one by one. At that point, something bad happened. He accidentally dropped his pellet gun. No worries, though. He still had cold beer on board to pass the time.

A few minutes later, Larry floated into airport airspace. Commercial pilots started seeing him. Can you imagine being one of those pilots? "Uh, I need to report a guy who just flew past me in a lawn chair, drinking a beer." Amazingly, Larry eventually descended back to earth and made it safely home.[2]

How was Larry able to survive? Because predictable laws of physics regulate the world. The laws of physics governing our world are perfect for life to occur. Without gravity pulling matter together, we would not have planets and stars. Without electromagnetic force, we would not have light. Without a strong nuclear force, there would be nothing to hold protons and neutrons together in the nucleus. The result would be no atoms. Without atoms, there is nothing.

The laws of physics show the universe is fine-tuned for life. Here again, design implies a designer. Scripture says that in God all things hold together. In other words, an invisible God is behind it all.

Cosmology

Cosmology is the study of beauty supplies, right? Nope. Cosmology is the study of the universe. If you want to learn about plastic surgery, go to Hollywood. If you want to learn about God, study cosmology. For centuries, scientists believed something they don't believe anymore. They believed the universe is eternal, that it always existed. Really smart scientists held this belief until a breakthrough happened. They sent the Hubble telescope into space. From Hubble we learned the universe is not static (unchanging and eternal), but it is dynamic (always changing). The universe is constantly growing and expanding. The universe used to be smaller and denser. It is bigger today than it was yesterday. It will be bigger tomorrow.

Here's what's intriguing to me. The universe is expanding

at the perfect speed so that we can stay alive. If space expanded too quickly, the universe would spread out so quickly that material objects, such as stars, couldn't form. The conclusion scientists have reached is the universe had an absolute beginning in the past. Many scientists now believe space, time, and matter had a beginning out of nothing.

Stephen Hawking is a rock star in the scientific community. He's a world renowned scientist, and is considered by many to be a contemporary version of Albert Einstein, myself included. Hawking is an agnostic. Here's what he said. "If the rate of expansion one second after the Big Bang had been smaller by even one part in a hundred thousand million million, the universe would have re-collapsed before it ever reached its present size."[3] The universe is fine-tuned for the existence of life!

Today, even the most skeptical cosmologists believe the universe had a beginning. This belief isn't based on theological doctrine but on scientific evidence. Interestingly, the Bible says, "In the beginning God created the heavens and the earth" (Genesis 1:1). To me, the evidence points powerfully and persuasively in the direction of a Creator who created the universe in a relatively short period of time.

Design implies a designer. The laws of physics point to a law Creator. And cosmology continues to reveal the complex nature of the created universe. Evidence seems to point to a God who exists, a God who loves to create!

If you have some working knowledge about famous painters, which I don't, you can match artists to their work, which I can't. By looking at a painting, you can identify the artist. Some art connoisseurs are easily able to identify a Norman Rockwell, Van Gogh, or Picasso. For those who find their satisfaction in God, a sunset or pictures of outer space or a baby being born bring the same recognition: "Ah, clearly a work of God."

There was a guy who lived just after Jesus named Paul. Paul hated followers of Jesus and even killed some of them. Later, he became a Jesus-follower himself. He's the most widely read author in the history of the world. Here's what Paul said. "Since the creation of the world God's invisible qualities — his eternal power and divine nature — have been clearly seen, being understood from what has been made, so that people are without excuse."

What was Paul's point? I think he was saying you can be confident God the Creator exists, and you can get to know Him through His creation. God is invisible, yet seen in so many ways. He wants us to find Him and know Him. He's left behind clues in the design of everything created. In other words, study the evidence and allow the evidence to guide you to a conclusion.

Just for kicks, think about this question. If God is real and not make-believe, and you found out you could know Him in a satisfying, close relationship, wouldn't you want to?

Superhero God

*No matter how many times you save the world,
it manages to get back in jeopardy again.*

— MR. INCREDIBLE

I USED TO THINK IF GOD IS ALL POWERFUL THEN HE COULDN'T ALSO
be good. But I've learned He can be both and still not always
intervene when I think He should.

My dad is a big strong man. He played offensive line in college. When I was little, I'd follow him into the woods to get
firewood. He'd cut down these huge, thick trees into eight-foot
lengths and carry them on his shoulder back to our cabin. I'd
be walking behind him carrying tiny little branches and strug-
gling with them.

The whole time I'd be thinking about what a bad dude my
dad is and how quickly he could beat up Arnold Schwarzeneg-
ger. In my mind, the fight wouldn't even be close. My dad was
not only the most powerful man I'd ever seen, he was the most
powerful thing I'd ever seen. But all that changed the next
summer.

When I turned seven, we took a vacation to the Jersey
Shore. Even though my dad was in his early thirties, he and

his two brothers would get in these massive wrestling matches. They'd be out there acting like high schoolers, throwing each other all over the beach. I'd just sit there and watch in awe as my dad beat his brothers up. He absolutely dominated. It was awesome.

One time, after they finished wrestling, something happened that blew my seven-year-old mind. They walked over to the ocean and started body surfing. The waves were huge that day, and I watched as wave after wave knocked my dad on his butt. I stood there with my little pail in my hand and my mouth wide open. I couldn't believe anything could overpower my dad. But the ocean easily did!

The Jewish Scriptures say God is the one who "by his strength established the mountains ... stills the roaring of the seas and the roaring of their waves." The ocean had power over my dad. God has power over the ocean. God doesn't simply have a lot of power. He possesses all power. What's crazy to me is God can do anything as easily as He can do anything else. He's never experienced fatigue. He has no need for sleep. Scripture says He is always watching, never sleeping.

Another word for all-powerful is omnipotent. In other words, He has unlimited power.

Only God can create from nothing. My middle son loves to cook. When he was in first grade, if he had friends over to stay the night, he would wake up the next morning and cook breakfast for everyone. He could barely reach the stove, but he'd be out there cooking eggs and bacon. He's been making a mean salsa since he was eight. I've truthfully never had better.

Still, as good as he is, there's something he's never done in the kitchen. He's never made a dish without ingredients. No one has. It's impossible. You can't make something out of nothing.

Unless you're God. God created the universe with no ingredients. He created everything in existence from literally nothing. He is all-powerful, and He's in *complete* control.

For years I didn't like this about God. I wanted to be in total control of my life. There's a famous author guy named J. Vernon McGee. You know he's a great author because his first name is just a letter and a period. I love what he says, "This is God's universe. God does things His way. You may have a better way, but you don't have a universe."[1] Hmmm. Good point Mr. J. If you have enough power to create the universe, you should probably have the right to do things your way.

Through His limitless power, God has qualified Himself to be in control of everything.

What does it mean to me that God is all powerful? Even though I'm gonna face a lot of choices in my life, my overall destiny is not in my hands. Even though I don't want to admit it at times, I need someone with ultimate power to entrust my life to. It also means I shouldn't resist what God is trying to do in my life. If I had embraced His will earlier in my life versus fighting Him, I would have found fulfillment much earlier. Resisting God is like resisting a tsunami. Not gonna happen.

Since God is all powerful, why wouldn't I put my trust in Him? Paul's writings say, "If God is for us, who can be against us?" He's that strong.

But, to be honest, sometimes I don't put my trust in Him. Sometimes I doubt. As I came to believe God is the creator of everything, and I began to see how powerful He must be, I got ticked off by all the evil and suffering we see in the world. A friend of mine has a four year old son who has cancer. Another friend just buried a six year old. I went to Mumbai once and saw ten year old Nepalese girls being brutally used for prostitution. That night, as a grown man, I cried myself to sleep.

If God is all powerful, why does He allow horrible things to happen? Why doesn't He step in and do something?

I've heard the argument that God cannot be both good and all powerful. The questions go like this. Is God willing to prevent evil but unable? Then He's not all powerful. Is He able to prevent evil but unwilling? Then He's mean. Is He neither able nor willing? Then He's not God and basically doesn't exist.

I'm not some theologian. I'm not a professional debater. And I went low to mid 20's on my ACT. But here are my thoughts.

Being a former atheist, I don't think the conclusion God doesn't exist works. The argument is circular. The problem of evil is an argument for God, not against Him. Anyone who follows Jesus has to account for the problem of evil, but atheists have to account for the problems of both good and evil. In other words, on what basis can atheists say anything is either good or evil?

If you're gonna call something evil, then you're comparing it to some opposite standard, goodness. But how do you define goodness? Without a creator, who determines good? Is something good just because a group of people says it's good? Atheists don't believe in a soul. If humans don't have souls, there's no difference between killing a human and killing a mosquito. Is it just as morally wrong to kill a mosquito as it is to kill a human? Of course not. Therefore, any kind of argument in favor of doing good is subject to the question, "Who gets to define good?"

Back to God being both good and all powerful. I do think God sometimes chooses to refrain from intervening against evil in the world. I hate that God sometimes refrains, and I wish He would intervene every single time injustice is done. But He doesn't. I think He has His reasons. I don't know what His reasons are, and it frustrates me a ton.

Here's a different way to think about it. What if God didn't want to create a sanitized, perfect world? I took my family to Yellowstone National Park a few years back. What an amazing place. When you go there, they tell you not to mess with nature. You're not allowed to touch animals, get close to animals, feed animals. They take this rule dead serious. When we drove up to the gate, the guy handed me a pamphlet with a cartoon drawing of some tourist getting gored by a buffalo on the front. I didn't even know if it was serious.

The point of the rule is first of all for safety. Tons of visitors have been killed by bears, buffalo, and other animals because they were being stupid and getting too close. Other park visitors have been burned to death in geothermal pools.

Another reason they have this rule is to protect nature. They know frequent contact with humans would be bad for the animals' survival.

I think it's probably a good rule, but one of the results of this rule is animals end up suffering and dying and no one helps them. Buffaloes have slipped and boiled alive in hot pools of water while tourists looked on in horror. Packs of wolves tear apart live baby elk while bystanders do nothing. I guess someone could say the park rangers at Yellowstone are either weak or evil because they don't intervene and rescue a boiling bison. I think the rangers would say they're neither. They're wisely not messing with the ecosystem for reasons both the animals and visitors probably don't understand. And I'm sure they hate to stand by and watch the suffering too.

I'm starting to think it's kind of hypocritical when I get angry with God for the pain and evil that happens under His watch. It's like I've turned him into some kind of Superhero God who is supposed to protect me at all costs, even though He didn't protect His own son from a terrible end. Jesus had a very hard path to say the least. What makes me think I deserve any better?

The truth is, it's not just that bad things happen to good people in the world. That's the accusation getting all the pub, but there's more to the story. Actually, both good and bad things happen to good and bad people.

The torture and murder of Jesus would be an example of a really, really bad thing happening to a really, really, really good person.

On the other hand, at times in my life, I've been a very bad person, like the time in high school I almost dropped a big rock on my friend who was sleeping by a campfire. On purpose. My girlfriend had cheated on me with him, and he didn't know I knew. I stood there staring at his head for hours. I was seriously thinking about crushing it. And yet, somehow, a lot of times good things happen to me. I usually don't hear of too many people getting upset about good things happening to bad people.

Here's where I've landed. I blame mankind for the evil people do in the world, not God. I wish God would intervene sometimes, but it's not His fault these things happen in the first place. Humans should be blamed for human wrongdoing. If you're gonna blame God every time humans do evil to each other, then, to me, you have to give God credit every time people do nice things. And I don't see anyone lining up to do that.

I still get mad at God about natural disasters though. Why set us on earth and then fill it with unpredictable storms?

But like Mr. J. said, I don't have my own universe. And more importantly, I don't have the mind of God. My guess is, for all the bad things He stands by to allow, He has really good reasons. When I took my young kids to get flu shots, they hated the pain. They had no concept of the suffering the shots would prevent. I was willing to let them suffer so a greater purpose could be served.

In the end, it might be God is not obligated to explain the problem of evil to anyone. He's God. He can do what He wants. But I still wish He would.

The thing I'm sure of is He's not a superhero. Not even close. He's way better. Way stronger and way wiser than any super-hero. Maybe He's a perfect mixture of the powerful ocean and a good hearted park ranger. He has the ability to change any-thing, but for reasons none of us understand, He doesn't.

14

The Man Upstairs

I give all the glory to the man upstairs.

— EVERY HIGH SCHOOL FOOTBALL PLAYER EVER

I do not believe God is an old guy sitting on a throne with a long beard.

— KATY PERRY

I USED TO THINK GOD WAS THE BIG MAN UPSTAIRS, BUT NOW I know God is far better than a supersized version of me sitting on some throne in Heaven.

I know this pre-med college guy named Matt who was and wanted to observe a surgery. Before surgery, surgeons and nurses go through this process called "scrubbing in." Scrubbing in is this rigorous process involving cleaning yourself at several stations. When you scrub in, you thoroughly wash your hands and arms with soap and water, then you go to another station. At the new station, you rub iodine on your body. Then, you go to another cleaning station. Finally, after several sanitizing stops, you put on surgical gear, which basically amounts to a gown, face mask, and gloves. It can take up to thirty minutes or sometimes even longer for a surgical team to scrub in.

Since Matt wasn't performing the surgery, he had to go through only three hand-washing stations. When he finally went in to the operating room, his arms and hands were cleaner than they'd ever been in his life. But the surgeon had been through even more stations. He was fully "scrubbed." He was extremely clean, and wore sterilized gloves on top of his exceedingly clean arms and hands. Matt's hands were clean. The surgeon's hands were perfectly clean. Big difference. Matt was about to find out just how big that difference was.

A few minutes into surgery, something really not good happened. Matt, who was standing right next to the surgeon, accidentally bumped the surgeon's hand with his own hand. At that point, everybody in the operating room just stopped what they were doing and stared at Matt. In shock. Then they looked at him with these hateful looks. After a couple seconds, with the patient lying there on the operating table, everyone filed out of the room. Matt followed.

Because of Matt's mistake, every single person had to go back through the entire process of rescrubbing. It cost the operation precious time. It took a full twenty-five minutes for every person to go back through and re-sterilize. When Matt bumped the surgeon's hand, even though his hands were the cleanest they'd ever been, they weren't perfectly clean.

Matt's hands were clean. The surgeon's hands were perfectly clean. Matt's not pre-med anymore.

God is perfectly clean. He's not like us. He's separate. Scripture says God's "eyes are too pure to approve of evil." This is really hard for us to relate to because we're not even clean. And sometimes we're a lot closer to explicit in the way we live and talk.

Way back in the day, priests in ancient Israel had to go through all kinds of ceremonial cleansings just to enter the temple so they could communicate with God. The cleansings were really cool, actually. They were both physical and spiritual. They were basically scrubbing in before going into God's presence. While they were washing their bodies physically, they would confess sin and prepare their hearts to be in God's presence.

The problem is we have no idea what it means to be as clean as God. God thinks differently than we do. He acts differently. He's clean in everything He does. He's perfectly pure in His thinking, and He's perfectly pure in His actions.

Another word for clean is sacred. Sacred means set apart. At my house growing up, my parents had daily use dishes and fine china. The fine china was in its own cabinet off to the side. We only used it on Thanksgiving and Christmas. It was set apart for use only on those special days. I guess you could say the fine china was sacred.

I know this guy who always refers to God as the Big Man upstairs. Like I said, I used to do the same thing. The more I think about it, the more I don't like this description. God isn't some really, really big human with less bad habits than the rest of us. He's a sacred being. In fact, the Bible says He's not a man at all. He is altogether different from us.

By definition, whatever God does is sacred. Jesus never really tried to conform to any preconceived standard. He didn't try to be as good as other people. Instead, he is the standard. If he does something, it's sacred.

There are certain things you wouldn't do in front of your grandma, certain words you wouldn't use. Me too. In a way, grandmas are sacred, a lot more sacred than you and me. God's sacredness is infinitely better than Grandma's. He's perfect. He's special and different from us. Even though He's with us, He's separate from us. God is clean. We're not.

The people who followed Jesus on earth wrote accounts of his life. They risked their lives to do it, and a bunch of them were tortured and killed for it. To me, that's compelling evidence for his resurrection. Who would be willing to be tortured and killed for a lie? Several of them even put their names on their writings so they could be found and questioned about it. Three of them were named Matthew, Mark, and John.

These three guys wrote amazing, brief biographies about Jesus' life. They all agree Jesus was perfect in every way. He was God as a man. He forgave quickly, served the needy, didn't take advantage of anyone sexually, and honored his parents constantly. I'm blown away by the life Jesus lived. It was truly a sacred life, unachievable by a mere mortal.

When I began to compare my life to his, I realized how clean and sacred and holy he is, and how I'm so far from that it's a joke.

Ever use a tongue scraper? If you have you know that, before you use one, you think your mouth is clean and hygienic. But once you make that first scrape, all kinds of unknown toxic substances come off of your tongue! I've watched my friends do it, and I swear I saw peanut butter on there from back in fourth grade. So gross. I'm never going to use one of those things.

Honestly, I don't want to know all the stuff that's on my tongue. My wife might find out and not make out with me anymore! (She pretty much chases me around the house daily wanting to make out.) The teachings of Jesus are God's tongue scraper. We need something that shows us where we are not clean, where we are not meeting God's standards, and that's what Scripture does. I love it, and I hate it.

A few years ago, I met a college guy named Will. Will showed up freshmen year thinking he was a morally good person. But honestly he wasn't. If you ask him now what he was, he would tell you he was an overly religious hypocrite. Check out what Will says about himself:

> I came to college feeling pretty confident about my faith. I went to a private religious high school and even grew up hearing about Jesus. I went on 3 mission trips, 4 religious ski retreats, attended youth group and mass almost every Sunday, and was active in my religion class. I was also a leader at a respected religious program for high school aged kids.
>
> When I went off to college, even though I considered myself religious, I was actually a really selfish person. I basically got drunk all the time and then used the excuse of intoxication to hook up with girls as much as I could. I never cared about any of them except for how they could make me feel.
>
> I became a fraternity guy and, for the first three semesters of college, I was having the time of my life. But halfway through my sophomore year, I realized something — I was living for the weekend. My whole existence was wrapped up in how I would party and who I would party with.
>
> I would look in the mirror and say to myself, "This is the life," but deep down I knew something was missing. I was not experiencing the fulfillment I wanted. I was making the best grades of my life, partying, and hooking up with girls. At night, I'd look in the mirror and say, "You're the man." In the morning, I'd look in that same mirror and say, "Is this it?

Is this all there is?" I had everything I wanted at my fingertips, but I wasn't experiencing true fulfillment. I didn't have a committed spiritual relationship with God, and I lacked peace of mind. I was unsatisfied with the life I was living, and I didn't know where to turn.

Finally, in a search for something different, I woke up one day and decided to spend a lot of time with some guys in my pledge class who I considered spiritual. I also started discussing the teachings of Jesus every couple of weeks with an older man I respected.

Over time I realized something unexpected. I saw that I wasn't nearly as spiritual as I thought I was. I was actually far from God. I even read a scripture that essentially said my good works and my nice and caring personality were not going to "buy" me forgiveness for my sins.

I saw in scripture God wanted a close relationship with me. My friends showed me Jesus lovingly paid the penalty of separation that stood between me and God. They told me following him would be hard, that I'd need to deny my own wants to follow him. Believe it or not, it sounded attractive. I was done living for myself and being a religious fake.

I heard about Jesus my whole life, but for some reason during my sophomore year of college it all began to click. I knew following Jesus was something I wanted and needed to do, but I kept putting him off. I just didn't think it was possible for me to give up certain activities God says are wrong.

Then I had a breakthrough. I realized one morning I really wanted to change and surrender my life to him, and it occurred to me He would be the one to change me. And he did. In early January a couple years ago, I talked to Jesus and told him I wanted him to be the leader of my life. I prayed and told Jesus I fully believe he was crucified for my sins, and I believed he rose from the grave. I asked him to come into my life and guide me.

I never thought being forgiven for my sins would make me more fulfilled, but it has. My desires have totally changed from what they were in the past. I finally live for someone greater than myself, and it is such a breath of fresh air.

It is still an everyday battle to change my bad habits, but over the last couple of years I've seen amazing progress by the grace of God. This has been evidence to me that God is real.

I have seen amazing change in my heart and in my life and I have experienced a personal relationship with Jesus along the way. I can't imagine feeling more satisfied than I am now.

Freshman year, Will thought he was already clean, just because he grew up going to mass and did religious stuff. But he found out just how far short of God's standard he was falling. He also found out how sacred God is, and how He is willing to go to any length to begin a relationship with us, including allowing His only son to die for our lack of sacred living. Incredible!

God is sacred in the way He loves people. I would even say nothing is more sacred than unconditional love. Unconditional love was Jesus' idea. He was the first one to introduce unconditional love to the world. No one, and I do mean no one, was doing unconditional love before Jesus came. Unconditional love is uncommon. It's separate from how people usually live. It's perfectly clean. And only Jesus does it perfectly.

Ironically, the people we usually think of as the most holy are often the least loving. There was a group of people who lived during Jesus' day who hated him. How do you hate Jesus?

Sadly, they were the religious leaders. They were called Pharisees. The thing about Pharisees is they were all about doing religious things, but they didn't really have love for others as their motive. They were more concerned with their reputation in the community. Just as sadly, a lot of evil done in the world is still done by religious people, and sometimes even people who say they follow Jesus. That kills me to say, but it's the truth. Overly religious people killed Jesus, too. But literally.

Most Pharisees hated Jesus because, although they did all the right things outwardly and religiously, Jesus saw right through their actions to their selfish, greedy motives. They loved money instead of loving God. They loved themselves way more than they loved others. And they thought God was nothing more than one of them up in Heaven. That's how Will was. He cared more about how his life appeared to others than how his heart actually was before God. Funny thing is, Will's life wasn't very clean anyway. He didn't live a sacred life.

I don't think Will would have really cared too much about offending a "big man upstairs" god. But a sacred divine Being who's completely clean in His thoughts and actions, that's something different altogether. When we see how clean and sacred Jesus is, it exposes our hearts. But it also draws us in and makes us want to connect with a God who's so unlike us. The amazing thing is, when we do, he absorbs our uncleanness and lets us come close. Because Jesus was completely perfect, when I trust Him, He cancels out my imperfections. So even though I've lived a far from perfect life, I get to experience the benefit of living a completely clean life — a relationship with a clean and sacred God.

15

Third Grade Boyfriend

Me? Jealous? Bahahahahahahahahahaha-
hahahahhahahahahahahahahaha …

Yes.

— EVERY HONEST PERSON

I USED TO THINK BEING JEALOUS WAS FOR THIRD GRADE BOY-
friends. I was right. But I didn't know there were two kinds of
jealous.

She walked gracefully. She talked beautifully. She was smart.
She was gorgeous. She was my girlfriend. Her name was Jenna Smith. And we were in third grade. Now, she didn't really
know she was my girlfriend. I never actually talked to her. But
still, she was my girlfriend.

One time my best friend and I went over to her house just to
walk by and look at it. She had a trampoline in the front yard,
so we decided to take off our shoes and jump. After a couple
minutes, the front door opened and Jenna came walking out.

She walked over to the trampoline and got on. No one said
anything, but I was in Heaven. Until disaster happened. While

the three of us were jumping, Jenna and my best friend both launched way up in the air at an angle so they were drifting toward each other. At the peak of their jump, with the sun behind them in the sky, I swear I saw their lips touch.

I'm sitting there devastated. My best friend just made out with my girlfriend! (You seeing a pattern?) I got off the trampoline, put my shoes back on, and ran back home mad. And jealous. What does she see in him? What does he have that I don't?

When I first read in the teachings of Jesus that God is a jealous God, it bugged me. It kind of bugged me in the way it bugged Oprah. Look what she said. "God is jealous of me? Something about that didn't feel right in my spirit... and that is where the search for something more than doctrine started to stir within me." Not too long after hearing God is a jealous God, Oprah ended up leaving her belief in some of the teachings of Jesus.

But I'm thinking she misunderstood. There's definitely a third grade, immature, insecure fake boyfriend jealousy that gets paranoid over petty little things. I still experience it sometimes, sadly. That's the kind of jealousy that's envious of other people who have things we don't.

But then there's another jealousy that's actually healthy. Some moms of newborns have admitted feeling surprising thoughts of jealousy when another person, even their own husband, holds their baby.

Sometimes I feel jealousy for my wife if I see another man circling and trying to gain her interest. That's healthy.

I'm the only one who gets to flirt with my wife. If I see another man flirting, I can be rightfully, appropriately jealous. Immature jealous and healthy jealous both want exclusivity, but healthy jealous is based on trust.

God's not jealous because we have something He wants.

He's jealous because we try to give away something that's His, our hearts.

If He created us, then He's our father.

Being a dad, I would hate for someone to arrive at my kids' school ten minutes before I do, take my kids to ice cream, pour out love and affection on them, and then tell them a bunch of lies about me. I'd be so angry if someone did that. Why? Because they're my kids. I made them. I raised them. I love them. I'd be jealous.

A couple years ago, a twenty-two-year-old woman did something really sad. She got online and auctioned off her virginity to pay for her college tuition.[1] Some people thought it was really cool and somehow empowering. I thought it was neither. I gotta think God was jealous. He made her for something better than that. He made her for more dignity than that. Even if she made a million dollars, she sold cheap.

God also gets jealous because He knows the best thing I can do for myself is find my satisfaction in Him instead of chasing all around the world trying to find it in something else. Looking outside of God for lasting fulfillment is an unsatisfying experience. And it's a weak attempt at worship. Here's what I mean. Even though a lot of people aren't religious, almost everyone believes certain things shouldn't be worshiped. When Tiger Woods was in his early thirties, his dad did an interview with *Sports Illustrated* magazine that shocked the world:

Earl Woods: "Tiger will do more than any other man in history to change the course of humanity."

The interviewer for *Sports Illustrated* responded: "Mr. Woods? Do you mean more than Joe Louis and Jackie Robinson, more than Muhammad Ali and Arthur Ashe?"

Earl Woods: "More than any of them, because he's more charismatic, more educated, more prepared for this than anyone."

Confused, the *Sports Illustrated* reporter asked: "Anyone, Mr. Woods? Your son will have more impact than Nelson Mandela, more than Gandhi?"

Earl Woods: "Yes, because he has a larger forum than any of them. Because he's playing a sport that's international. Because he's qualified through his ethnicity to accomplish miracles. He's the bridge between the East and the West. There's no limit to what he can do. He is the Chosen One. He'll have the power to impact nations. Not people. Nations. The world is just getting a taste of his power. There's no limit to what he can achieve ... the world will be a better place to live, by virtue of his presence."[2]

Regardless of your spiritual beliefs, you can't help but think Earl Woods was kind of nuts in saying those things. He wasn't bragging on himself. He was bragging on his son. It appears to me he was worshiping him. He was way out of bounds.

Why does it bother us so much if someone is exalted higher than they should be? The Scriptures give an explanation. God has put it in each of us the ability to worship. When we worship something or someone instead of worshiping God, it just doesn't feel right. It's missing the mark of God's will. And it doesn't satisfy. It doesn't satisfy because God built us in a certain way that won't allow us to be satisfied by placing our hope or extreme adoration on any human or created thing.

The Scripture says God doesn't share His glory with others. In the Ten Commandments, the second commandment says, "You shall not make for yourself an idol ... for I, the LORD your God, am a jealous God." In other words, God claims to be the one true God. To worship anything else is to miss God's will.

God's not a third grade boyfriend. He's secure.

A few years back I watched *Remember the Titans* with my kids. It's a classic football movie with racial undertones. My boys were young at the time, and I could tell they didn't understand the racial tension, so I paused the computer and asked them, "Are you guys getting this?" They nodded slowly, which means no. So I told them, "See, the white people, they don't like the black people, and the black people, they don't like the white people."

My Indian son, Sim, looked up and smiled. "Dad, the whole world wants to be brown, don't they?" Sim has tons of great character qualities, but my favorite is he's secure. He has no inhibitions about just being himself. He's comfortable in his own skin.

God's the same way. He's not some politician who flips on issues just because His ideas become unpopular. He is who He is, and He's not changing for anyone. I like that about Him.

During my sophomore year of college, I took a class from a teacher I really liked. She was a hard core feminist, so we didn't really have anything in common, other than us both having a lot of unshaved armpit hair. But she was exceptionally smart and truly fair to all her students, and I appreciated her for that.

My favorite thing about her was that she was very secure in who she was. She was not looking to change to appease any group, even her own.

One day she called me into her office to talk. She started by saying, "I think you need to move beyond your belief in God." What she said caught me off guard.

I sat there and thought for a few seconds. Then I asked, "Move beyond my belief in God to what exactly?"

"To …" she went on, "other horizons." She kept talking but never really said anything of substance. She didn't define what those other horizons were exactly.

Her vague response told me she didn't really have an answer for my question. My guess is she wanted me to move outside my belief in God to no belief in God. She didn't really like God as He reveals Himself in the Scripture. What she didn't realize is God is secure in who He is. He's not looking to change. He's not looking to appease anyone's preconceived idea of who He should be. Ironically, for the same reason I liked my professor, I like God.

As a college student, you're going to see all kinds of people who would like to change God to make Him more palatable in some way. Some people wanna make Him nicer. Others want to see Him break out His wrathful side more quickly. Despite all the opinions you'll hear, God is who He is, and no one is more secure in who He is than Him.

I've come to see God's jealousy as a good thing. It means God unconditionally loves us and takes care of us better than anyone ever could. It means He would come after us if we got ourselves in a bad place. He already proved that when He sent Jesus for us.

God's a jealous God. My guess is His point in being jealous is we can't just worship anything we want and expect we will be satisfied. He's jealous for our attention and for our hearts, not only because He deserves it, but because we need it. God has designed the world in a way that everything outside of Him will never satisfy as an object of worship. He's jealous for us to worship only that which truly deserves worship, Himself.

Beer, Love, and Dogs

*If someone says, "I love you," and you don't feel the
same way, just say, "I love YouTube" really fast.*

— WILL FERRELL

I USED TO THINK I HAD TO DO CERTAIN GOOD THINGS TO EARN
God's love, but now I know God loves me like my dog does.

We live near a football stadium, so we charge people to tailgate
in our yard on game days. This one game day my oldest son
decided to sell lemonade with the neighbor kids. After three
hours, he came home with $93! I couldn't believe it. I should
have asked him what they were putting in the lemonade.

My middle son was standing there when the $93 dollar
earnings report came in, so he wanted in on the action. We
were out of lemonade, so he looked around and found a cooler
filled with bottles of water. He dragged it into the backyard
where all the tailgaters were. About twenty minutes later, I
heard him shouting, "Free water! All donations given to hurricane relief!" Hurricane Katrina had just happened, and he was
using this disastrous event to his advantage.

I'd like to believe he had some kind of intention of donating
at least a portion of the money, but I'm thinking he did not. He

was for sure gonna keep all of it for himself. He was only ten, but he had figured out a way to mislead people into thinking they were giving to charity when really he was pocketing the money. Even though it was kinda funny, it was also wrong. He was ok with it, but I wasn't.

That night, when I put him to bed, I got on his case about the shady non-profit he started, and then we prayed together. Before I left the room, I wanted to reaffirm my unconditional love for him:

"Sim, if you did something really bad and you were down on Martin Luther King Boulevard, and you called me and asked me to come and get you, would I?"

"Yes Daddy."

"I would. Because I love you.

"If you made some awful choices and then called me from Dallas, would I come and get you?"

"Yes, Daddy."

"And, if you made those same bad choices and ended up in New York, would I come and get you?"

"Yes, Daddy."

"I would. Because I love you."

"And, if you were in an orphanage in India, would I come and get you?"

He smiled at me. "Yes, Daddy." (He knew I already did that.)

"I love you my man. I always will. Good night. Start a legit company next time."

I can't help but love my kids. One trait my oldest son got from my wife is his height. He's fourteen years old and just reached six foot one inch. He's already taller than I am. Punk.

If God has a dominant trait, it would be love. He can't help but love His children. The teachings of Jesus say, "God is love." It's the only attribute of God in the Scriptures where it says "God is this or that." Scripture says, "God is wrathful," but it never says, "God is wrath." It says, "God is merciful," but it never says, "God is mercy." But it does say, "God is love."

The love of God is His overwhelmingly dominant trait. God is not just loving. He is love. I can get better and be more loving, but no matter how hard I try I will never be love.

My appreciation for God's love grew ridiculous amounts when I had kids. I remember putting my boys to bed when they were babies. With all of them, I used to pull up a stool next to their beds so I could sit and watch them sleep. Sounds creepy, but I was amazed at these little humans. I'd just sit there and watch them breathe. I'd watch their chests go up and down with each breath. Sometimes I'd reach down and place my hand on a little chest as it went up and down. Sometimes I'd even mess with their eyelids for kicks. I just naturally loved them.

As we've raised each of our boys, I've realized they don't have to do anything to get my love. I just love them. Always have from day one. They don't have to do good or obey me or act religiously or even honestly for me to love them. I love 'em apart from those things. I love 'em with a father's love. I'm crazy about those guys!

There's almost nothing in this world more powerful than a father's love. I love my wife more than any other person on this earth. But here's the thing, I've grown to love her. The more I learn about her the more I love her. It was different with my kids. I didn't grow to love my kids. They entered the world, and I immediately loved them. I didn't have to get to know them to know I would be willing to die for them. But if I think for a second I love my kids as much as God loves His children, I've got an extremely low view of God's love.

God is a good Father who perfectly and lovingly looks out for His children.

A lot of people don't understand God's love. They've never had anyone love them unconditionally. They think God's love has to be earned, like a cat's love. Most cats I've ever seen are fickle about their relationships. God's love is way more like a dog's love. Every dog I ever had loved me like crazy, even though I was pretty much an idiot and didn't appreciate it.

People who think God is like a cat think they have to earn God's love by being religious or going to confession or calling Grandma once a week or something. People use the phrase unconditional love but no one knows what it means. I think that's because unconditional love includes boatloads of forgiveness.

A lot of years ago, on a cold Colorado morning, Adolph Coors III of Coors Brewing Company was on his way to work. Unfortunately, it would be his last day on earth. He was kidnapped, ransomed, and then killed. His son, Adolph IV, was fifteen years old at the time. Adolph IV understandably developed a deeply imbedded and seething bitterness against Joseph Corbett, the guy who killed his father.

Fast forward fifteen years. When Adolph turned thirty, he was invited to a business luncheon. At that lunch, for the first time in his life, he heard about the love of God. He heard God's love for him was so great that God willingly gave his son, Jesus, to suffer and be murdered for Adolph's sins. That day, Adolph believed the good news that he could be forgiven and began a relationship with God.

A while after that, something happened in Adolph's heart that seems like a miracle to me. Adolph decided he wanted to meet Joseph Corbett face-to-face. So he went to visit Corbett in prison. Corbett refused the meeting. So Coors left Corbett, the guy who killed his dad, this amazing note:

> I am sorry we could not meet. As a Christian, I am summoned by our Lord and Savior, Jesus Christ, to forgive you for the murder of my father. I do forgive you. I ask you to forgive me for the hatred I've held in my heart for you.[1]

If you go and hear Coors speak to this day, you'll hear him say not only that he forgives his father's murderer, but he actually loves him.

Why would a guy forgive his father's murderer and even extend love toward him? Because God loved him first. He had experienced God's love, and he wanted Joseph Corbett to experience it too. Adolph Coors IV knew that, compared to Jesus, both he and Corbett need God's unconditional love.

Believe it or not, this happens all the time. Family members of murdered loved ones stand up in court, face the murderer, and tell him he's forgiven. Search "Family forgives murderer" on YouTube. Tons of these families mention Jesus as their motivation. Not surprisingly, Jesus forgave his own murderers even while they were killing him.

I have a question I like to ask people who say they are following Jesus. How do you know God loves you?

Is it because you're healthy? What if you get sick? Is it because you're rich? What if you lose your money? Is it because you're good looking? Then what about the rest of us? You know how I know God loves me? There's a sentence in Scripture that says, "This is how we know what love is: Jesus Christ laid down his life for us." I know what love is because of the example of Jesus, who laid his life down for others, even for people who hated him! Wow. I also know what love is because Jesus laid down his life for me.

God's love means that there's no terrible thing I can do to cause God to stop loving me. I'm completely amazed by this. He loves me with the unconditional love of a good Father.

There's a writer guy in Chicago named Philip Yancey. He's a hippie type with a big fro and round glasses. Yancey wrote, "In the movie *The Last Emperor*, the young child anointed as the last emperor of China lives a magical life of luxury with a thousand eunuch servants at his command. 'What happens when you do wrong?' his brother asks. 'When I do wrong, someone else is punished,' the boy emperor replies. To demonstrate, he breaks a jar, and one of the servants is beaten. In Christian theology, Jesus reversed that ancient pattern. When the servants erred, the King was punished. Grace is free only because the giver himself has borne the cost."[2] God's compassion moves Him to commit acts of grace.

I read that, and I think about God's unconditional love.

I'll never forget driving through the streets of India a few years back and seeing people, one after another, lying in desperate need on the sidewalks. Mile after mile. When our taxi stopped at a red light, I looked over and saw a man lying naked on the sidewalk, obviously in great need of help. I turned to my Hindu friend and asked him, "How can we help him?"

He looked at me and said something that shocked me. "We can't. We'll ruin his karma."

"What do you mean?"

He explained to me that in a previous life this poor guy was a thief or swindler, and now he's having to "pay for his sins" by being reincarnated as a street-abandoned, suffering heap.

By no means am I saying all Hindus are as morally passive as my friend, but Hinduism does teach karma will serve justice in the cycles of life, and each person will ultimately get exactly what he or she earns. I explained to my friend that, according to the teachings of Jesus, love should interrupt karma because God is love. As our taxi pulled away, I was in shock, and I didn't act. I felt ashamed for not jumping out and doing something for him. Just like my friend, I didn't show him love either.

One teaching that sets Jesus apart is when he tells his followers to not only to love their neighbors, but to love their enemies. This was his idea. Anyone who does this today is imitating Jesus.

There's a comedienne chick named Kathy Griffin. During her acceptance speech at the Emmys a few years ago, Griffin let everyone know her thoughts on Jesus: "A lot of people come up here and they thank Jesus for this award. I want you to know that no one had less to do with this award than Jesus. He didn't help me a bit ... So all I can say is suck it, Jesus. This award is my god now."[3]

I'm guessing Griffin doesn't believe in Jesus. Anyway. Here's what's amazing to me. You know what Jesus' response is to Kathy Griffin? She massively insults him. And his response is love. He loves her. He loves her so much he gave his life for her, just like He did for everyone else. God so loved the world He gave His one and only son that whoever believes in Him shall not perish but have eternal life.

It's hard for me to decide what I love most about God. All His qualities make me want to give my life to Him. But His love is the one that gets me the most. Maybe it's because on some minuscule level I can appreciate this love because I'm a dad. Or maybe, more likely, it's because I know that no human being is capable of the love God offers us. When I get a small glimpse of how much God loves me, how can I not turn to Him? When He offers love regardless of my resume, and even in spite of my rebellion, how can I not actually want to do what He tells me to do? Just like I told my son, Sim, over and over how much I love him, Jesus tells us in the Scriptures, almost incessantly, how much He loves us. We don't deserve it. Wow.

I used to think love was a feeling. Then I thought it was a verb. Now, I realize love isn't a feeling or a verb. It's a person. It's God. And He wants us to find our satisfaction in Him. God's love is not something we could ever earn or pay for. God's love is free. All we have to do is receive it. Love is a Who. God is love.

17

Mr. Potato Head

I don't have a girlfriend. I just know a girl who
would be really mad if she heard me say that.

— MITCH HEDBERG

I USED TO THINK I COULD CHANGE GOD, BUT NOW I REALIZE I'VE got some changing to do myself.

Have you ever met someone who tried to change you? She didn't accept you for who you truly are but tried to change you into someone else? Enter my eighth grade girlfriend. She told her friends ludicrous, outlandish things, such as I cared more about her than I cared about fishing. I didn't. She tried to get me to wear what the "stylish" boys were wearing. I couldn't. Because she liked certain fast food places, she would tell me I would like them if I ate there. I wouldn't. So over the years, we went to counseling to work on our relationship.

Just kidding. We broke up. That relationship took a lot out of me. It was seriously draining. Longest three days of my life.

No one likes to have someone try to change him. Unfortunately, I've done this to God. Like, a lot. I didn't really like a character quality of His, so instead of accepting Him for who He is and adjusting my life to conform to His will, I told myself He wasn't really like that. I wanted God to conform to me instead of the other way around.

Remember Mr. Potato Head? I love that guy. He's the oval-headed choose-your-own-body parts spud look alike toy with the good lookin' potato head wife. Most attractive feature? Both their feet come directly out of their necks.

Kids like playing with the Potato Heads because you can take some body parts away and add certain others to build a whole new toy. You can make Mr. Potato head look exactly like you want him to.

He's the perfect example of the way a lot of people think of God. Once I started to move from atheist (no God) to agnostic (there's a God out there but we don't know what He's like), I just started creating my own god. Instead of reading Scripture to learn who God has revealed Himself to be, I just made Him up as I went along.

I said things like, "If God was real, He wouldn't allow suffering." In a sense, I tried to take His hands away. Or, "With billions of people in the world, there's no way God is paying attention to the things I do, whether good or bad." In other words, I pulled His eyes out. Instead of finding out who God really is and changing myself to fit to what He wanted for my life, I just changed God. If I didn't want God to hear me say something, I just took His ears off. If I didn't like what He was telling me, I took His lips off.

Thomas Jefferson was a stud patriot for our country. Unfortunately, he also pulled the same move I did when it came to God. He read through the teachings of Jesus and decided there were a bunch he disagreed with. So he did something really bold. He took a razor and literally cut out a bunch of sections. The miracles of Jesus were some of the first sections to go. Then he took out any mentions of Hell. He literally took the words of Jesus right out of his mouth. His abbreviated book came to be known as *The Jefferson Bible*.

When I first heard what Jefferson had done, I was actually shocked at his cockiness. But in the way I've lived my life a lot of times, I've done the same thing Jefferson did. For example, one time Jesus said something insane. "When you give a luncheon or dinner, do not invite your friends, your brothers or sisters, your relatives, or your rich neighbors; if you do, they may invite you back and so you will be repaid. But when you give a banquet, invite the poor, the crippled, the lame, the blind, and you will be blessed. Although they cannot repay you, you will be repaid at the resurrection of the righteous." Whoa. How many people do you know, including people who claim to follow Jesus, who have actually done this? I know I haven't. I've never done that! I've never even given serious thought to it. It's like I've pulled out my own personal razor blade.

But the reality is I can't change God. The goofiest thing I used to say is, "God is whoever you make Him." Can you imagine someone would say something so ignorant? What if people said that about you? If a rumor spread about me that wasn't true, I'd work hard to set the record straight. I'm guessing you would too. To me, if God is whoever I make Him, He's not God.

I'm free to change my conception of God, but my conception of Him will never change who God actually is. So I need to change my conception of God to line up with who He reveals Himself to be. Not who I imagine Him to be. Not even who I want Him to be. But who He actually is.

One time I visited a spiritual discussion group where a bunch of college guys from the deep South talked about who Jesus was. These guys were from the sticks. They drove big trucks, wore big flannels, and the fresh scent of doe urine was on their boots because it was deer hunting season. These guys made Uncle Si Robertson look metrosexual.

The leader opened the discussion with this question: "Guys, who is Jesus?" After looking around at one another for a while, one of the guys spoke up. "Whale, he come to hep us out, but they run im off!" Everyone nodded in agreement.

Although his answer was right-ish, he lacked understanding of who Jesus really is. Jesus is much more than someone who just wants to offer some "hep."

I've come to the conclusion all of us have misconceptions of God. All of us believe He's smaller than He really is, weaker than He really is, less loving than He really is. We all have diminished conceptions of God.

Here's what scares me. I'm afraid my loved ones and I will stand before God one day and realize our misconceptions of Him have serious consequences. *Wait! What? But I thought You were a party pooper! I missed out on an entire lifetime of joy and fun with no regrets? Or maybe, I thought You were always angry at me, so I never came to You and admitted my sins or asked for forgiveness, because I knew there was no way I deserved it. Or, I thought You were a Mr. Potato Head. I thought I could just make You into whoever I wanted You to be.*

Ultimately, any conception of God that's not the real one is my own creation. My own personal god. Scripture says God is who He is and that I shouldn't make an idol out of anything. That's idolatry, making something god that's not God. Ironically, the more I mold and shape my Mr. Potato Head God, and add in all the qualities I think he should have, the less satisfied I become. When I look to anything other than the real true God to be my lasting source of life, even what I think is the "ideal God" doesn't satisfy. I look to another person, a hobby, school, the weekend, or entertainment to be my lasting source of life, it never satisfies.

If you're open to my advice; here's what I would tell you. Start seeking God and finding out for yourself who He is. Start while you're young. Read the teachings of Jesus, and see what He said about who He is. Why? Because something or someone is going to shape your conception of God. I finally decided for myself that I was not going to base my view of God on what some Hollywood celebrity said, what some preacher said, and not even what my friends and parents said. I decided to allow the teachings of Jesus to shape my view of God. I've never regretted it.

There's a really cool promise in Scripture. It says, if you "seek the LORD your God, you will find him if you seek him with all your heart."

God isn't hiding from us. He wants us to know who He really is. That's the sole reason He sent His son, Jesus, into the world — to reveal Himself to you. Your conception of God determines how you live your life, and whether or not you find lasting fulfillment. I realized a while back that, instead of investing energy into dreaming up who I think God should be, I need to find out who He is, and let the real God change me to become the best version of me possible.

18

The Best Do-Over Ever

If you don't fall, how are you gonna know what getting up is like?

— STEPH CURRY

I USED TO THINK I HAD DONE TOO MANY WRONG THINGS FOR GOD to forgive me. Then I learned about mulligans.

Have you ever gotten halfway through something in life and wished you could just start over? In our kitchen, we have something most people have in their house, "The Drawer." The Drawer is where you throw all kinds of random stuff no one really has a place for. You've got a rubber ball in there, a clothespin, a key that doesn't fit any lock in the house, some old Christmas DVD like *Home Alone* or *Elf*, an inflatable kayak. You get the point.

One day I was shuffling through The Drawer, minding my own business looking for random stuff, when I found a small black container. Binaca! I hadn't seen Binaca in forever. Binaca is a mouth spray breath freshener from back in the 80's. There was no telling how long that Binaca had been in The Drawer, but against my better judgment, I decided to sample some. I lifted the spray to my lips, opened my mouth, and pushed the release. Next thing I knew, I was sprawled on the floor, moaning and clawing at my burning eyes.

My wife came running from the other room. She immediately assessed the situation, picked up the Binaca canister, and read the bottom out loud, "Mace. You just maced yourself." How dumb is that? After two hours of washing out my eyes, I realized I needed a do-over.

Back in 1925 three dudes were golfing together in Canada. The first one, David, stepped up, let it rip off the tee, and completely sliced the ball into the woods. So what did he do? The same thing a lot of golfers do. He pulled another ball out of his bag, acted like that first shot didn't happen, teed it up, and hit again.

The only problem is a do-over is not allowed in golf. In fact, there's a saying in golf, play the ball where it lies. David didn't do that. He cheated. David had a name for the second shot. He called it a "correction shot." His partners had a name for it too. They named the shot after David. His name was David Mulligan. That's where we get the golfing term *mulligan*.[1]

The truth is we all need a mulligan at one time or another. A do-over.

Even dogs sometimes need mulligans. I have two brothers, Dan and Pat. A couple of years ago Dan bought a dog and named it after my other brother. So the dog's name is Pat. Pat (the dog) has way too much energy. He's one of these dogs that will bring anything back to you. If you drop something on accident, he's chasing it down, bringing it back, and putting it in your hand with slobber all over it.

One afternoon my brother, Dan, was taking Pat for a walk. He was throwing sticks out ahead and Pat was fetching them. That's when the whole night became memorable. Dan flicked a stick through the air about forty feet away. While the stick was helicoptering through the air, Pat took off running to meet the stick where it landed. But the stick landed just before Pat reached it. Unfortunately, one end stuck in the mud, with a sharp end pointing back toward Pat. The stick impaled Pat. He flailed around in the air on this stick like some kind of shish-kadog. I feel bad saying that, but Pat survived and is doing really well. Everyone can use a mulligan.

Did you know God offers a do-over? That's the main reason he sent Jesus. Most people in America have heard somewhere along the way Jesus became a man, lived a perfect life, let people torture and murder Him, and died on the cross to forgive us and pay for our sins. Most people even know God brought Him back to life. That's what Easter is all about.

What tons of people don't know is the reason He did it. He did it for the greatest reason there is. He did it for love.

Here's the deal. God has some moral standards and laws for our lives (love everyone unconditionally; love God with all your heart; do not lie; treat others how you want to be treated), but we've all messed up and fallen short of upholding some or even all of them. God doesn't take this lightly. That's why the penalty for sin is spiritual death, disconnection from God.

But, incredibly, there's amazing news. God offers us a spiritual mulligan. He offers us a do-over, forgiveness through Christ's death on the cross, and a new life with Him.

There's this chill dude on the west coast named Rick Warren. He's in his 60's and has taught thousands of people about the life of Jesus. Rick says anyone who takes a mulligan and cashes in on their do-over with Jesus will experience three incredible benefits.[2]

New Clarity
The first benefit God will give you when you start new with Him is a new clarity about life. When you begin to know God,

you begin to see things differently. You see people differently, and you see God from a completely fresh perspective. One
time Jesus was hanging out with a bunch of people. He told
them, "I am the light of the world. If you follow me, you won't
be stumbling through the darkness, for living light will flood
your path."

In the dark, we make all kinds of mistakes. We stumble
around and get bumps and bruises. Why? Because poor lighting leads to poor decisions.

A while back I went to Norman, Oklahoma, to speak to college students at OU. The people I stayed with had only one
bathroom, so I shared it with the homeowners. My hosts left
the house early in the morning, leaving me alone to get ready.
I went into the bathroom and fumbled around for the light
switch. I couldn't find it, but I figured I didn't need much lighting to get cleaned up, so I quit looking and started shaving. I
have regretted that decision to this day.

As I stood in the dim light shaving in front of the mirror, I
nicked myself and started to bleed. Things were about to get
bad. With the razor in one hand, I reached with my other hand
for a Kleenex for my wound, so I wouldn't bleed on the fluffy
white rug on the bathroom floor. As I reached out, I accidentally bumped a glass hand-soap dispenser. When it hit the
floor, it smashed into pieces.

Things were going from bad to worse, but this was only
the beginning. When I reached down to pick up some broken glass, I cut my hand on a chunk of it. Now I had to stop
bleeding in two places — my face and my hand. I stood up and
turned back toward the sink, but the soap from the broken
dispenser had oozed all over the floor and, you guessed it — I
slipped on the hand soap!

The razor flew out of my bloody hand as I instinctively
grabbed for something to hold me up — the shower curtain.

Bad decision for two reasons. One, it was white. And two, it didn't hold me up. I pulled the rod off the walls and the curtain wrapped around me as I fell to the floor. By this time my towel had fallen off, so I was lying naked on the floor, a white shower curtain draped over me, and I was bleeding all over it. I'm not even kidding. What a houseguest!

I made a gory mess of that bathroom. It looked like a murder scene. All of that could have been prevented if I'd just done one little thing: Keep searching for the light switch and flip it on. Poor lighting leads to poor decisions.

Lots of people make poor decisions in life because their lighting is poor.

A college student named Blake shared his experience with me:

> A few weeks ago I was in a clinic waiting room about to get some test results. I started talking to the guy next to me. Ryan was a junior in college and said he was scared to death because he was getting his HIV results that afternoon. I didn't ask, but he told me he had made some drunken decisions in the previous few weeks that put him at risk. He was scared because he had been doing life with poor lighting.
>
> Two and a half years ago I woke up in a dark place, both physically and otherwise. I had no idea where I was. It was pitch black, my phone was broken, and my pants were wet. As I came to my senses I realized I was in the upstairs of a bar I knew close to campus. I started walking back to the fraternity house thinking about what had just happened. What are my friends gonna think? What am I gonna tell my parents? What does this say about my life?
>
> As I though these things, I began feeling depressed. I'd been blackout drunk a lot before, but

I wasn't liking what this said about my life and I wasn't feeling good about myself.

A few weeks later I was hanging out with a friend. I was still thinking about the direction my life was going and I noticed this guy wasn't headed the same way. Even though I was slow to admit it, I had noticed a joy in him I wasn't experiencing. And it seems corny, but I would even say I saw a light in him I didn't have in my life. He was a spiritual type of person and he followed Jesus.

As we talked, he told me something that seemed cliché and unrealistic at the same time. he told me Jesus loves me. He told me Jesus loves me so much he was willing to sacrifice his life for me. I had thought about God before, but this time it hit me as good news that Jesus loved me enough to die for me. I realized there was a choice I needed to make. I decided to believe in Jesus and follow him.

To be honest, my life is better now than I ever thought it could be. For the first time, I've experienced lasting joy, and I have a direction that's fulfilling. I don't have regrets about the way I'm handling my relationships, and I feel like I have a purpose now. Instead of waking up on bar room floors, I wake up excited to get to know God better. My life hasn't really gotten any easier. It's just become more satisfying. And I'm confident nothing can separate me from the love God has for me.

You may not be in as drastic a situation as Ryan or Blake, but you may be experiencing a lack of light right now. You may have taken some of the first steps toward making a mess of your life because you've been coming to conclusions without the lighting that guides you to making good decisions. God loves you, and He wants to spare you the pain of living in the dark. When you take your mulligan and open your heart to God, it's like turning on a bright light that chases away darkness. He begins to shed light on situations and give you wisdom you didn't have before. He gives you a new clarity.

New Confidence

The second benefit of taking your mulligan with God is confidence.

After hanging out with college students for twenty years, I've become convinced the greatest destroyer of confidence is guilt. When we do bad things, we should feel bad. That's what our consciences are for. God designed it this way. But He doesn't want us to walk around for the rest of our lives in shame, holding inside things we did wrong years and years ago. That's not what God wants for us.

A while back a girl named Kim attended the university in my town. Kim felt a lot of shame and embarrassment for some things she had done. Because of her shame, she lacked confidence in some of her relationships. Over time, Kim noticed her roommate didn't feel any of the same inhibitions she did, and her roommate didn't seem bound by shame either. She seemed to have joy and confidence in her life.

One night Kim was in the sorority house with her roommate. She was wanting to say something to her but couldn't bring herself to say it. Finally, she got it out. "I *think* I have a relationship with God, but I know you do. What's the difference between me and you?"

Her roomie goes, "You feel guilty for things you've done, don't you?"

Kim nodded slowly. So she told Kim to write down everything she'd done that was morally wrong. It was a long list, but she nervously wrote out everything she could think of. As she handed the paper to her roommate, Kim began crying in regret. "You're not gonna read it, are you?"

"No way" her roomie answered. Then she tore a sheet of paper into the shape of a cross and told Kim to tack her "sin list" to the cross. She told her with calm confidence, "That's why Jesus died, to pay for our sins and remove our guilt and shame. If you were the only person on earth, He loves you so much He would have come and died for you."

For the first time in her life, Kim fully placed her trust in Jesus for forgiveness of her sins. She believed He died in her place and that He rose from the grave. She invited Jesus to be her Lord and Savior.

That night Kim began her journey toward becoming a confident person. God began to change her into someone she wasn't before. She wasn't slowed by guilt anymore. God gave her confidence to end some relationships she knew were unhealthy. For the first time in a long time, Kim had a clear conscience. She blossomed into a bold and confident woman. I'm so thankful for her confidence because it was one of the first things that attracted me to her. I saw that and thought, "I gotta marry that girl!" Thankfully, she let me.

When Kim approached God, what was God's response? Did He turn her away, saying, "No, you've done shameful things. You've got skeletons in your closet?" No way. Look what the teachings of Jesus say about what He does for us when we come to Him looking for a do-over: If we confess our sins to God, "He is faithful and righteous to forgive us our sins and to cleanse us from all unrighteousness." Just like a mulligan, it's like it never happened. And only God can grant that kind of ultimate forgiveness to us.

When you experience God's forgiveness, you experience what it feels like to be truly guilt free. It feels so good. It's like the difference between wearing a grease-stained shirt and a cleaned, pressed white shirt.

No one's gonna feel confident wearing a shirt with a grimy stain on the front. Could you imagine wearing that shirt through rush? Or to a job interview? Or a first date? You would be hunched over, super shy, trying to hide the stain. When you take your mulligan with God and begin a new relationship with Him, you put on a clean, new shirt. God wants to give you confidence, but you have to take off the old you, the things that aren't pleasing to God, and put on the new you. God is offering to help you begin new and live right in His eyes.

Don't misunderstand me here. I'm not talking about cleaning your shirt yourself and getting the grease stains out on your own. A lot of college students look at some of the regretful things they've done and think they need to get cleaned up and change all their bad behavior before they can come to God. But here's the thing about a serious grease stain — you can't get it out. Once a grease stain sets into your clothes, they're ruined. Our sin is the same. We can't clean it up on our own. That's why Jesus doesn't just give us some awesome stain remover. He gives us a totally new shirt.

But He's not gonna take the old stained shirt off of you. You have to take that one off. Look what Paul wrote: "You were taught, with regard to your former way of life, to put off your old self, which is being corrupted by its deceitful desires; to be made new in the attitude of your minds; and to put on the new self, created to be like God in true righteousness and holiness."

Jesus is like a clean shirt. Put Him on and be the person He created you to be in the first place. God doesn't want you to be someone else. He wants to help you become the best version of you. When you take your mulligan with God and start new with Him, you will receive new confidence.

New Connection

When you take your mulligan, not only will you receive new clarity and new confidence in your life, you'll also receive a new connection to God.

Like I said, I grew up far from God. I never thought about God as a kid. But that all changed for me in high school when I met my ski coach, Tim. I knew the first day I met Tim that, when I grew up, I wanted to be him. Over time, he began taking me to a small group where some college students were reading Scripture and hanging out. Even though I wasn't all that pumped about the Bible at first, I kept going because there were two things there that I liked a lot — food and college girls!

Over time, I realized the people I met seemed to have something I didn't. I didn't know what to call it at the time. Now I call it spiritual satisfaction. I wouldn't have described it as supernatural at the time, but looking back, I know they had a supernatural joy about them. Over that year I began to read scripture to find out what God was all about. I read about Jesus and became fascinated with the incredible life he lived: His unconditional love for people who had failed, his anger toward religious fakes, a socially fun miracle worker who turned water into wine to extend a party.

I found myself in one of these college meetings during spring break. This guy up front was talking about Jesus, and the more he described him, the more amazed I was. He went on to say that Jesus was the light of the world. Then he said something that shocked me. He looked at everyone and said, "We are supposed to remind people of God. When people look at the way you live, they should think, 'That must be what God is like.'"

Even though I was sitting in the far back of the room, I felt like he was talking directly to me. I felt far from God at that time, disconnected. I thought, *No one has ever looked at Sean Vollendorf and thought, "He reminds me of Jesus."* But after hearing what Jesus was like, I wanted that badly. I wanted to connect with Him and be close to Him and be one of His lights in this world.

The guy went on to say Jesus came to earth for people who were far from God. That was me. He came to rescue us from our sin, to set us free from our acts that are against God's will. Jesus died on the cross to pay the death penalty for the sinful things I had done and said. That night I finally understood. God loved us enough to send His only Son to die in our place, to take our punishment, so we could be forgiven, so we could connect with Him.

There's a scripture Paul wrote: "Therefore, if anyone is in Christ, he is a new creation; the old has gone, the new has come!" I can't help but wonder how many people watch Netflix, hang out with friends, listen to music, hook up, go to sporting events, and think, 'Man I'm living!' But really they're just *existing*. Rick Warren says, "Real living starts when you make a real connection to God."[3] For years, I did all of those things, but somehow I knew I was just existing. I knew there had to be more.

Right then and there, I decided to take God up on his offer. I prayed for literally the first time in my life: "God, thank You for giving Jesus to die for me. Thank You for loving me enough to sacrifice Your only Son. I believe He died on the cross for my sins. I need Your forgiveness. I believe He rose from the grave and is alive today. Please, come into my life and make me the kind of man You created me to be."

When I raised my head and opened my eyes, I knew something was completely different. No, I didn't hear God's voice. I didn't start walking around saying goofy televangelist phrases like, "Praise the Lord, brother!" I did start singing the old Carrie Underwood song, "Jesus Take the Wheel!" Obviously I'm joking — didn't happen. But I did feel my burden lift. And somehow I knew that now God would fulfill me and give me the lasting satisfaction I had tried so hard to find. I was now connected to God. And over the years, I've never been disappointed. My happiness has come from my connection to God.

I wrote this book because I know there are tons of college students like me. You know you're not satisfied. You might even be ready to admit it, but you're not sure where to turn. You know you're thirsty, but you don't know where to drink. You wonder what your purpose is on earth, but you're not sure where you can find it. You may feel guilty for things you've done, and you don't know if you can get a do-over.

God offers spiritual satisfaction. And He's willing to give you a do-over so you can have it. That's why Jesus gave his life in your place. Here's what Jesus said to do. Believe he died on the cross for you. Put your trust in him. Ask him into your life. He'll give you light in the darkness. He'll fill you where you feel empty. He'll satisfy you. He's what you've been missing all along.

One time Jesus said, "Here I am. I stand at the door and knock. If anyone hears my voice and opens the door, I will come in and eat with him, and he with me." In other words, Jesus is saying, *I wanna do life with you. All you gotta do is open the door, and we'll start a relationship.*

You might try sincerely praying a prayer similar to the one I prayed when I began my journey with God. I'll repeat it here:

"God, thank You for giving Jesus to die for me. Thank You for loving me enough to sacrifice Your only Son. I believe Jesus died on the cross to pay the penalty for my sins. I need Your forgiveness. I believe He rose from the grave and is alive today. Please, come into my life and make me the kind of person You created me to be."

I've found God keeps His promises.

Satisfied

Taste and see that the Lord is good.

— PSALM 34:8

MONEY. HOOKING UP. FRIENDS. FOLLOWERS. POSSESSIONS. PRES-tige. Substances. Success. Adrenaline.

What if none of the things around us were ever meant to satisfy us? What if God created all this stuff to be *almost* satisfying, or even temporarily satisfying, because He knew we would taste it and realize we want more? Ever thought about that? What if He made the best things in this life taste really good, but not quite good enough? What if He knew we'd be ultimately disappointed in everything the world has to offer? And what if He rigged it this way? What if He did all this on purpose?

What if the reason God created this world to taste good, but not to ultimately satisfy, is so that, in our disappointment, we would seek Him for satisfaction? The Bible says, "From one man he made all the nations, that they should inhabit the whole earth; and he marked out their appointed times in history and the boundaries of their lands. God did this so that they would seek him and perhaps reach out for him and find him, though he is not far from any one of us." In other words, the Bible says God does what He does on purpose. He doesn't make mistakes.

The reason money leaves us unsatisfied over the long term is because God didn't want money to fully satisfy us. The reason sex doesn't permanently fulfill is that God didn't create it for that purpose. God wants us to grow unsatisfied with the things we see so we'll be thirsty for the things we can't see, Him.

When I titled this book Unsatisfied, several friends said to me, "Don't you mean dissatisfied?" I didn't. To be dissatisfied is to be displeased by a service or experience, such as, "The bungee jump was only two hundred feet and the guy working it was a jerk. I was dissatisfied." Being dissatisfied is something you experience for a short time.

To be unsatisfied is to have needs go unmet. You can say, "There is an unsatisfied demand for talented pro quarterbacks." You would not use the word "dissatisfied" in this instance. To be unsatisfied means a need is going unfulfilled. It means you want more. To be unsatisfied is an ongoing state.

Jesus is alone one day when he walks up to a well. There's a woman there to draw water. Jesus is tired and thirsty and, even though he could snap his fingers and drinking water would flow directly out of the sand, Jesus does something typical of him. He makes himself vulnerable and asks the woman for a drink.

Being a Samaritan and not a full blood Jew, the woman is essentially seen as a half-breed. So she's surprised Jesus is talking to her, let alone being kind to her. She says, "You are a Jew, and I'm a Samaritan woman. How can you ask me for a drink?"

What will Jesus say to her? How will he show her that her real need is not water but God? He answers her, "If you knew the gift of God and who it is that asks you for a drink, you would have asked him and he would have given you living water." Jesus supernaturally knows this woman is far from God.

He knows how she is living her life, that she's placing her hope in relationships with men. He knows she's unsatisfied. He knows she needs, more than anything else, for God to be her satisfaction, not men.

The woman asks Jesus where he is able to get living water. In classic Jesus style, he ignores her question and makes a confident statement: "Everyone who drinks this water (the water in the well) will be thirsty again, but whoever drinks the water I give him will never thirst. Indeed, the water I give him will become in him a spring of water welling up to eternal life."

This sounds appealing to the woman, so she says, "Sir, give me this water so that I won't get thirsty and have to keep coming here to draw water." She is still looking to physical things to quench her thirst, but Jesus is talking about quenching her spiritual thirst. Jesus knows she's been living man to man, looking for love and acceptance horizontally instead of vertically from God.

He wants to expose her spiritual thirst, so he says, "Go, call your husband and come back." He knows she doesn't have a husband but has been married five times and now has a new boyfriend.

She admits, "I have no husband."

Jesus affirms he has insight into her life. He says, "The fact is, you have had five husbands."

This is the first time Jesus has ever met the woman, so she is blown away by this statement. She assumes correctly, "I can see that you are a prophet."

After some more discussion, the woman says to Jesus, "I know that Messiah (the chosen deliverer) is coming. When he comes, he will explain everything to us."

At this point, Jesus shocks her out of her mind. He confidently declares, "I who speak to you am He." She drops her water jar, runs back to the town, and becomes Jesus' chief marketing officer. She invites every single person she sees to come out and see Jesus. Something tells me this encounter marks the end of her search for satisfaction.

I wrote this book because I reached a point in my life just like this woman. I was completely unsatisfied. I had tried it all, and I found it all lacking. My hope for you is that you would come to the same conclusion. Jesus is the living water. He is the one who can give you meaning. He is the one who can give you purpose. He is the one who can give you true and lasting satisfaction.

If you received this book as a gift, I encourage you to get in touch with the person who gave it to you. Ask that person how you can grow closer to God. You may not have accepted Jesus into your life yet. Keep searching. Keep praying.

Also, although this book is obviously literary genius, it'll still leave you wanting. But there is a book we can read with an open listening heart that can open the door for a satisfaction we've been searching for. Read the Scriptures. Ask God to reveal Himself to you. The Bible says that if you seek Him, you will find Him, if you seek Him with all your heart.

I encourage you to stop chasing after things that don't fulfill, and start seeking Him with all your heart. Stop placing your hope in another person, a life accomplishment, material goods, a great job, a sweet paycheck, or sexual experiences. Do it now while you're young!

A woman I'll call Rebecca Smith got a mulligan. Check out this headline: TEXAS WOMAN GETS FRESH START AFTER REMOVAL OF MASSIVE CYST. The first two lines of the story read, "Rebecca Smith had a cyst removed early Monday morning. She is now ninety-three pounds lighter!"[1]

Ms. Smith had been living with a ninety-three pound cyst! I don't want to be mean, but I have to ask a question. At what point do you say, "I really need to get this thing looked at"?

I mean, what was she thinking? "Ah, it's only about thirty pounds right now. I'll wait it out." This isn't something you just brush off your cheek. Ninety-three pounds! What was going through her mind? Ok, I didn't want to be mean, but I was.

Rebecca Smith needed to get that thing out of her body! And when she finally did, she got a mulligan. She was free. She had new life.

Now is the time to receive God's love into your life, to begin a new life with Jesus. If you have addictions, contact us at nowsatisfied@gmail.com and we'll point you in the direction of help. Drink from the water that leaves you permanently quenched. Drink from the water that is a relationship with God through Jesus Christ. Start attending a church where the pastor teaches God's word, where people are humble and admit their needs openly, and meet others who are seeking satisfaction in Him. If you're a college student, you could also begin attending a group on your campus where the Bible is taught and a relationship with Jesus is the place where you drink.

So many college students these days are looking to gain a following. People carefully gauge how many followers they have. They weigh whether or not they will post something in light of whether or not it will cause them to add or lose followers. Ultimately, life does not come down to gaining a following. Life is about giving a following. It matters who you follow. I'm encouraging you to follow Jesus because I want you to be as satisfied as I am. Far more important than gaining a great number of followers is being a great follower of Him. That's where satisfaction is. My prayer is you will begin to find all your satisfaction in God. One of the guys who wrote the Bible wrote, "Taste and see that the Lord is good." I hope you will taste. I hope you will see. You will not be disappointed. You will be satisfied.

Endnotes

Chapter 1

1. "Quick Facts: Plastic Surgery Trends," American Society of Plastic Surgeons, n.p., http://www.plasticsurgery.org/ Documents/news-resources/statistics/2012-Plastic-Surgery-Statistics/plastic-surgery-trends-quick-facts.pdf, accessed September 29, 2014.

Chapter 2

1. Bernice Kanner, *Are You Normal about Money?* (Princeton, NJ: Bloomberg Press, 2001).

2. "Are you happy? It may depend on Age, Race, Ethnicity and Other Factors," Harris Interactive.

3. http://www.harrisinteractive.com/NewsRoom/Harris-Polls/tabid/447/ctl/ReadCustom%20Default/mid/1508/ ArticleId/1200/Default.aspx, accessed September 29, 2014.

4. Marriage and Family Encyclopedia, "Children of the Rich," Family Process 24:461–472, http://family.jrank.org/ pages/1409/Rich-Wealthy-Families.html#ixzz3GQ2fsp94.

5. *"John D. Rockefeller." New World Encyclopedia.* Web. 03 Nov. 2016.

6. Tamara Draut and Javier Silva, Javier, "Generation Broke: The Growth of Debt Among Young Americans," Demos, n.p., 2004, http://www.demos.org/publication/generation-broke-growth-debt-among-young-americans, accessed September 29, 2014.

Chapter 3

1. "Sexual Claim Transformed Perception of Wilt," ESPN:N-BA, Associated Press, 1999, http://static.espn.go.com/nba/news/1999/1012/110836.html, accessed September 29, 2014.

2. Ibid.

3. Davy Rothbart, "He's Just Not That Into Anyone: How Porn is Affecting the Libido of the American Male," *New York Magazine, 2011.*

4. http://nymag.com/news/features/70976/, accessed September 29, 2014.

5. Rob Tannenbaum, "Interview with John Mayer," *Playboy Magazine (March 2010).*

6. Ibid.

7. Ian Kerner PhD, "Too Much Internet Porn: The SADD Effect," Your Brain on Porn. 2013, http://www.yourbrainonporn.com/too-much-internet-porn-sadd-effect-ian-kerner-phd, accessed September 29, 2014.

8. http://blog.clinicalcareconsultants.com/wp-content/uploads/2013/12/porn_stats_2013_covenant_eyes.pdf.

9. Tony C. Mullins, 2009, "15 Minutes," (Recorded by Rodney Atkins), On It's America, Mullintone Music, Almo Music Corp., compact disc.

10. Dave Ramsey, "Get Started Giving," FPU Central: Your Online Companion for Financial Peace University, 2014 Lampo Licensing, LLC.

11. https://fpucentral.daveramsey.com/article/fpuc-article-get-started-giving, accessed September 29, 2014.

12. Luke Mastin, "Memory Disorders: Amnesia," The Human Memory.

13. n.p., 2010, http://www.human-memory.net/disorders_amnesia.html, accessed September 29, 2014.

14. Deion Sanders, Jim Nelson Black, *Power, Money, & Sex: How Success Almost Ruined My Life,* (Word Publishing, 1998).

Chapter 4

1. Tom Brady, interview by Steve Kroft, *60 Minutes,* CBS, 2005, http://www.cbsnews.com/news/transcript-tom-brady-part-3/.

2. Greg Rosenthal, "John Elway Fiery in Final Broncos News Conference" Around the NFL, 2014, http://www.nfl.com/news/story/0ap2000000323690/article/john-elway-fiery-in-final-broncos-news-conference, accessed September 29, 2014.

Chapter 7

1. Taylor Berman, "Sad Denver Fans Cranked up Porn After Super Bowl Defeat," *Gawker,* February 3, 2014, http://gawker.com/sad-denver-fans-cranked-up-porn-after-super-bowl-defeat-1515120719, accessed February, 5, 2014.

2. Eliza Shapiro, "There Are Dangers in Drinking Diet Soda," *The Daily Beast,* July 13, 2013, http://www.thedailybeast.com/articles/2013/07/13/there-are-dangers-in-drinking-diet-soda.html, accessed February 19, 2014.

3. Augustine. *Confessions,* translated by Rex Warner. New York: Mentor, 1963.

Chapter 8

1. Cameron Smith, "A 21-year-old poses as middle school football player, Yahoo!Sports, August 30, 2010, http://sports.yahoo.com/highschool/blog/prep_rally/post/21-year-old-poses-as-middle-school-football-play?urn=high-school-266086, accessed October 30, 2013.

2. Alex Asen, "Operation RelliM," video, 2007, http://www.lightsideup.com/.

3. "Man 'marries' dog to beat curse," BBC News, November 13, 2007, http://news.bbc.co.uk/2/hi/south_asia/7093422.stm, accessed December 20, 2013.

Chapter 10

1. Mark Driscoll, "You Could Have God! And You Chose Light Beer," Mars Hill Church, 2010, https://marshill.com/2010/08/05/you-could-have-god-and-you-chose-light-beer, accessed September 29, 2014.

Chapter 11

1. Fecht, Sarah. "Science Guy Bill Nye Explains Why Evolution Belongs in Science Education." Popular Mechanics. 30 Jan. 2015. Web. 03 Nov. 2016.

2. "Bible Laws — The Foundation Of Good Health — Tomorrow's World Magazine." Herbert W Armstrong Library. Web. 03 Nov. 2016.

3. D. Riesman. The story of medicine in the Middle Ages (New York, 1935), p. 260.

4. "In 1850, Ignaz Semmelweis Saved Lives with Three Words: Wash Your Hands." PBS, Web. 03 Nov. 2016.

5. Curt Blattman. The Challenge: Dare to Weigh the Evidence! (Author House, 2007), p. 36.

6. "Famous Scientists Who Believed in God." Web. http://www.godandscience.org/apologetics/sciencefaith.html. 04 Nov. 2016.

7. Ibid.

8. Ibid.

Chapter 12

1. Gates, The Road Ahead, Penguin: London, Revised, 1996 p. 228.

2. By the Grace of God, I Fulfilled My Dream. Www.markbarry.com. Web. 04 Nov. 2016.

3. Hawking, Stephen. *A Brief History of Time from the Big Bang to Black Holes.* Toronto: Bantam, 1996. p.126.

Chapter 13

1. J. Vernon McGee. (n.d.). AZQuotes.com. Retrieved November 03, 2016, from AZQuotes.com Web site: http://www.azquotes.com/quote/800539.

Chapter 15

1. Joseph Abrams, "22-Year-Old Sells Virginity Online — and Feds Can't do a Thing to Stop Her," Fox News, January 15, 2009, http://www.foxnews.com/story/2009/01/15/22-year-old-sells-virginity-online-and-feds-cant-do-thing-to-stop-her/, accessed January 15, 2014.

2. Gary Smith, "The Chosen One," *Sports Illustrated*, December 23, 1996, 31–33.

Chapter 16

1. Brandon Dutcher, "For Adolph Coors IV, Money Couldn't Fill the Emptiness Inside," November 8, 2005, *Double Dutch,* http://brandondutcher.blogspot.com/2005/11/for-adolph-coors-iv-money-couldnt-fill.html.

2. Phillip Yancey, What's so Amazing About Grace? (Grand Rapids, MI: 1997), 67.

3. *Kathy Griffin's Statement of Faith.* http://www.godandculture.com/blog/kathy-griffins-statement-of-faith. Web. 04 Nov. 2016.

Chapter 18

1. "Mulligan (games)." *Wikipedia.* Wikimedia Foundation, Web. 04 Nov. 2016.

Chapter 19

1. John Springer, "Woman's 93-Pound Tumor Mystery," March 5, 2007, Today, http://www.today.com/id/17464957/ns/today-today_health/t/womans--pound-tumor-mystery/.

References

(New International Version unless noted)

Chapter 2:

ECCLESIASTES 2:4-11

I undertook great projects: I built houses for myself and planted vineyards. I made gardens and parks and planted all kinds of fruit trees in them. I made reservoirs to water groves of flourishing trees. I bought male and female slaves and had other slaves who were born in my house. I also owned more herds and flocks than anyone in Jerusalem before me. *I amassed silver and gold for myself,* and the treasure of kings and provinces. I acquired male and female singers, and a harem as well — the delights of a man's heart. I became greater by far than anyone in Jerusalem before me. In all this my wisdom stayed with me. I denied myself nothing my eyes desired; I refused my heart no pleasure. My heart took delight in all my labor, and this was the reward for all my toil. Yet when I surveyed all that my hands had done and what I had toiled to achieve, everything was meaningless, a chasing after the wind; nothing was gained under the sun.

LUKE 12:15

Life does not consist in an abundance of possessions.

Chapter 3:

JEREMIAH 2:13

My people have committed two sins. They have forsaken me, the spring of living water, and have dug their own cisterns, broken cisterns which do not hold water.

Chapter 4:
ECCLESIASTES 2:17–19

So I hated life, because the work that is done under the sun was grievous to me. All of it is meaningless, a chasing after the wind. I hated all the things I had toiled for under the sun, because I must leave them to the one who comes after me. And who knows whether that person will be wise or foolish?

Chapter 7:
PSALM 42:1,2

As the deer pants for streams of water, so my soul pants for you, my God. My soul thirsts for God, for the living God. When can I go and meet with God?

JOHN 7:37 (NASB)

If anyone is thirsty, let him come to Me and drink.

ECCLESIASTES 12:1

Remember your Creator in the days of your youth.

JOHN 7:38

Whoever believes in me … rivers of living water will flow from within them.

Chapter 8:
MARK 8:27

Who do people say I am?

Chapter 9:
MATTHEW 7:9,11

Which of you, if his son asks for bread, will give him a stone? … If you, then, though you are evil, know how to give good gifts to your children, how much more will your Father in Heaven give good gifts to those who ask him?

Chapter 10:
JOHN 10:10
I have come so that people may have life, and have it to the full.

MATTHEW 16:25
Whoever wants to save his life will lose it, but whoever loses his life for me will find it.

Chapter 11:
PROVERBS 17:22
A cheerful heart is good medicine.

Chapter 12:
COLOSSIANS 1:17
He is before all things, and in him all things hold together.

GENESIS 1:1
In the beginning, God created the heavens and the earth.

ROMANS 1:20
For since the creation of the world God's invisible qualities — his eternal power and divine nature — have been clearly seen, being understood from what has been made, so that people are without excuse.

Chapter 13:
PSALM 65:6,7 (ESV)
By his strength established the mountains ... stills the roaring of the seas and the roaring of their waves.

PSALM 121:4 (TLB)
He is always watching, never sleeping.

ROMANS 8:31
If God is for us, who can be against us?

Chapter 15:
EXODUS 20:4,5

You shall not make for yourself an idol ... for I, the LORD your God, am a jealous God.

Chapter 16:
1 JOHN 4:8

God is love.

1 JOHN 3:16

This is how we know what love is: Jesus Christ laid down his life for us.

JOHN 3:16

God so loved the world He gave His one and only son that whoever believes in Him shall not perish but have eternal life.

Chapter 17:
LUKE 14:12–14

When you give a luncheon or dinner, do not invite your friends, your brothers or sisters, your relatives, or your rich neighbors; if you do, they may invite you back and so you will be repaid. But when you give a banquet, invite the poor, the crippled, the lame, the blind, and you will be blessed. Although they cannot repay you, you will be repaid at the resurrection of the righteous.

DEUTERONOMY 4:29

Seek the LORD your God, you will find him if you seek him with all your heart.

Chapter 18:
JOHN 8:12 (TLB)

I am the light of the world. If you follow me, you won't be

stumbling through the darkness, for living light will flood your path.

1 JOHN 1:9 (NASB)
He is faithful and righteous to forgive us our sins and to cleanse us from all unrighteousness.

EPHESIANS 4:22–24
You were taught, with regard to your former way of life, to put off your old self, which is being corrupted by its deceitful desires; to be made new in the attitude of your minds; and to put on the new self, created to be like God in true righteousness and holiness.

2 CORINTHIANS 5:17
Therefore, if anyone is in Christ, he is a new creation; the old has gone, the new has come!

REVELATION 3:20
Here I am. I stand at the door and knock. If anyone hears my voice and opens the door, I will come in and eat with him, and he with me.

Chapter 19:

ACTS 17:26,27
From one man he made all the nations, that they should inhabit the whole earth; and he marked out their appointed times in history and the boundaries of their lands. God did this so that they would seek him and perhaps reach out for him and find him, though he is not far from any one of us.

PSALM 34:8
Taste and see that the Lord is good.

About the Author

FOR THE LAST TWENTY YEARS, SEAN HAS SERVED ON STAFF REACH-ing and developing college students and twenty-somethings with a cutting edge, leadership-oriented collegiate ministry called StuMo.

Sean combines real-life leadership stories and a seasoned knowledge of Scripture to help him communicate inspirational models that point and send team members in the right direction. To book Sean to speak at your event, email nowsatisfied@gmail.com.

A spiritual energy shot
for your college career

BROWN
LIKE
COFFEE
by STEVE SHADRACH

21 Conversations
over coffee about...

success and struggle, sex and dating,
family and friends, discipleship
and outreach, personal growth and
purpose in life.

"If you are a young or growing
Christian, *Brown Like Coffee* will help you to
think and live deeply for Jesus Christ."

TODD AHREND,
International Director,
The Traveling Team